Pass the Biscuit

By Gary Wright

Ashworth Press

Cover Design: Stephen Belliveau of Mark Bergeron Design; Bryon Lewis
Printed by: Heffernan Press

Ashworth Press
P.O. Box 91128
Springfield, MA 01139

ISBN: 0-9629703-0-1

Printed in the United States of America

"We should not care who wins Pee Wee hockey games. Rather, we should be devoted to developing young players and making hockey fun."

-Red Gendron
Assistant Hockey Coach
University of Maine

ACKNOWLEDGMENTS

I am indebted to several people for this modest undertaking. Being a coach and not a writer, I looked to my mother, Nancy, who has authored several books, for assistance. My sister, Catharine, and colleagues at work, Bruce Johnson and Dr. Blaine Stevens, chipped in with some helpful proof-reading. Staff secretary, Dolores McClelland, and A.I.C. grad student, Brenda Couchon, typed and re-typed the manuscript.

I would be remiss by not recognizing my assistant coaches, Paul Cannata and Larry O'Donnell. And, a special thanks to my players.

CONTENTS

FOREWORD

"One of the things that this sport can and should do for a person is to make him into a cultivated sportsman, someone who can mix with other people, who can analyze a situation, who is self-critical and self-disciplined - someone who is a human being in other words."

-Anatoly Tarasov
Russian Olympic Coach

The line between youth hockey being a good or bad experience is razor thin. There is so much that is positive: coaches who are in it for the players, coachable players who are team oriented, parents who have the game in perspective, supportive fans. There is a dark side as well: egotistical coaches with a warped sense of control, players who are selfish and poor sportsmen, parents who undermine coaches and push their children to be "stars," fans whose ugly behavior degrades the game.

It should be every player's right to play for a quality coach: a coach with a love for the game and a will to teach it, who encourages creativity and sees the person in the player. A player deserves to be guided by someone who is not afraid to lose. And most of all, a child needs a coach who is a strong role model. Many of us have performed for such coaches.

I remember Gordon Lull, the late postmaster of Potter Place, NH, father of three children, scoutmaster and little league coach. This short, spectacled man, who recycled old balls with white shoe polish, didn't know much baseball - neither did we. But he could relate to young people. If you played on Mr. Lull's team, you put your uniform on after school and wore it proudly around town because you just couldn't wait to get to the ballpark.

I remember Chris Norris, consummate prep school educator, former college hockey player, and a coach you wanted to play for. A strong believer in skill development, he would often tell us, "It's a great feeling to let go a nice wrist shot." I pass that, and other things he taught, on to my own players.

Then there was Spencer Wright, my coach, my father. A red-headed extrovert, who called team members (including me) by their last name, his greatest hockey gift was not what he taught me about the game, but his attitude about it. There was no pressure to play - I could walk away any time. My dad didn't live the game through his son.

And finally Jim Cross, teacher, connoisseur of classical music, bird watcher and past hockey coach at the University of Vermont. Disheveled in appearance and once described as looking like an unmade bed, his integrity and devotion to fair play was an inspiration to those he coached. In 1984 Cross left coaching, but for nineteen years his passion for the profession graced the game.

I pass this reminiscence along partly because it warms me to recall these people, but mostly to relate the positive effects that come from a very powerful influence - the coach. We are so much a product of our past, of those who have touched us along the way.

In the over 100 drills included in the "20 practices," some I have designed myself, most were picked up from various coaches and publications. It seems I learn from almost every coach I see and, in fact, all of the practice information in this book is a composite of ideas from many individuals. To that end, I hope in some way this book will help coaches to better coach, and players to better play.

A few winters ago on a frigid December afternoon, a group of us played pond hockey on black ice. It was a neighborhood game and people of all ages joined in. After competing for a while, we worked to set up a seven-year-old, who had been trying to keep up with us, for a goal. When it happened, the child was elated and everyone whooped it up. It was all quite simple: a kid shoots a puck between two boots and a few witnesses share his joy. There were no spectators to cheer or boo, no newspaper reporters to cover the event, no scorekeeper to record the point - just smiles on half-frozen faces, frozen in time.

QUALITY PRACTICES

"Where would you want your child to play? How about a team that plays 60 games with 25 practices. What about the team that has 60 meaningful, well-planned practice sessions and plays only 25 games? You don't have to be a genius to figure out on which team your child is going to improve the most. Take a stopwatch to the next game and time how long a player is involved in skating time on the ice. Chart the passes, shots, receptions, stops, checks, etc. If you believe that repetition of movements or skills will improve those movements or skills, you know under which situation your child will improve most."

-Wayne Orn, Founder
Hockey Coach's Newsletter

    This chapter discusses some components necessary for ensuring quality practices. An organized practice means everything to a hockey team. And it means so much to the player, for a carefully planned practice in a wholesome environment will enhance the player's development, and contribute substantially to the young person's having a positive attitude about the game.

Planning A Practice

Effective coaches are organized. Organization begins with a well-planned practice.

Design a long term practice plan for the season in outline form. It does not have to be overly detailed but should list general objectives for the year.

A short term plan involves the practice(s) coming up. The practice drills should reflect team needs and objectives at that particular juncture of the season.

Write practice up and keep a copy of all plans on file.

Create progression from week to week. It is important to begin with basic skills and drills, and gravitate to more advanced forms.

Progression, while necessary, should not be overdone. Variety is critical. Therefore, starting a season with three straight "no puck practices" may indicate progression, but at the expense of the player's interest. Spread the "skating only" drills over a period of weeks, so other activity can be included.

Practices often have different tempos - quick and hard working, flow oriented, slowed down and technical, light workouts, etc. As a general rule, coaches should keep less active practices to a minimum, as these tend to diminish the team's enthusiasm. The more effective practices will often vary in tempo.

Be careful in the design. Avoid boredom by injecting variety and challenge into the practice plan: i.e. there are many ways to do a 1 on 1.

When designing a practice drill, whatever it is, consider all that can go wrong. What kind of demonstration will be necessary? Should cones be used? Do players start on their own or on a whistle? Can they stay at the net for rebounds, or will there be another group coming? After shooting, to what line do players go?

The average drill should be 5 to 10 minutes in length; long enough to provide ample repetition for skill development, but short enough to avoid overdoing it.

Drill succession is important. For example, whenever possible, do drills that originate from a certain area of the ice, in sequence, for purposes of continuity and to save ice time.

Select drills of an appropriate level of difficulty so the player can experience success. By the same token, more advanced exercises have to be included to provide challenge for the individual. Many drills can also be altered to accommodate players of different skills, and variable learning speeds.

Include game-like drills and competition in the sessions.

Excite players with spirited drills so they will want to come back. Try to make practices as enjoyable as the games.

Incorporate a fun exercise for the end of practice. It sends players home on a happy note.

Researching Practice Ideas

Record new drills on file cards or in a notebook.

Purchase hockey books/videotapes. "U.S.A. Hockey," based in Colorado Springs, Colorado, or the "International Hockey Centre of Excellence" in Calgary, Alberta, Canada, are two organizations with wonderful information on the game.

Attend clinics/coaching achievement programs. Studying up on the game is invaluable.

Visit a summer hockey school in the area. Hockey schools generally employ individuals who coach for a living.

Observe practices at all levels - professional, college, high school, youth hockey, etc. Attend as many practices as possible to learn new drills and tips from other programs. There is something to be learned from everyone.

Coaches should self-design some drills. All it takes is creative effort. Drills can be dreamed up that will greatly enhance the practice plan. Beyond this, inventing drills can be a rewarding experience.

Props and Attire

It is advisable to be outfitted in sweats or an instructor's outfit. Street clothes tend to project an unprofessional image.

Each coach needs to have a copy of the practice plan on hand. There are different ways to do this: on a clipboard, taped to glove (can be reduced on copy machine), in billfold of hat, taped to glass, attached to lanyard, etc.

Every coach has a whistle.

If a clock is not visible, wear a watch.

Players dress in full uniform. Different colored jerseys for lines, and a separate color for defensemen and goaltenders, if possible.

Keep a playboard handy for diagraming purposes, but use it sparingly. Overuse results in player boredom.

Place water bottles in the bench area for proper hydration.

Have ample pucks (2 - 3 per player).

Have a dozen cones readily available.

Utilizing Assistant Coaches

Every head coach needs at least one assistant, preferably two. Assign one coach to the goaltenders.

Assistants are an invaluable resource. They should be utilized extensively and given specific responsibility. A head coach acting alone makes for a poor player-coach ratio and the players miss out.

The practice plan should be shared with the staff beforehand, so coaches are familiar with the practice and their responsibilities.

An assistant has to be in sync with the head coach. If a coach is introducing a drill, the other sets up cones, moves pucks, etc., so players will not be waiting. Anticipation and pre-practice planning is the key.

One function of an assistant coach is to pull players aside for individual instruction. Assistants must be active, not standing around.

An example of effective delegation by a head coach would be to designate an assistant to oversee defensive play, and consequently allow the assistant 10 minutes of each practice to work exclusively with the team in that area.

After practice, analyze the session with the assistant coaches.

Value the input and contributions of assistants. Look upon them almost as co-coaches.

On occasion, let the players hear a fresh voice. Invite guest instructors to attend practice - a figure skater can teach power skating, a goaltending specialist might work with goalies, an old pro can pass on tricks of the trade, etc.

Maximizing Ice Time

Ice time is precious and should never be wasted. Practice must start as soon as ice is available and the hour utilized fully.

Review drills in the lockerroom before the team takes the ice. Chalk talks are not necessarily a substitute for on-ice demonstrations or instruction, but they allow players to better conceptualize the exercise(s). Thus, less is said on the ice and more gets done.

Do some light stretching (flexibility) off ice, especially if ice time is limited.

Incessant on-ice talk bores players. It's that simple.

Condition team members to help with pucks, cones, etc.

Insure a minimum of standing in line and a maximum of active participation. Keep lines and drills moving, but be cognizant that certain activities necessitate a proper work/rest ratio.

If the drill involves lines at opposite ends of the rink, two coaches can explain things at their respective ends. Gathering the entire group at mid-ice for a drill explanation is often unnecessary and wastes time.

Never talk to one player while the entire team waits. Players will begin to take offense at the interruption in play. One coach can quickly deal with the individual, while the other attends to the group.

Stations and splitting the team at both ends is beneficial. It makes for a good player-coach ratio and keeps everyone active.

Consider sharing the ice with another team, on occasion. It will double the ice time.

Coach's Professionalism at Practice

A good coach is an educator. Two essential attributes in teaching are communication and motivation. The message must get through to the players and they must be motivated to deliver on it.

Arrive a half hour before practice. Getting to the rink early allows time to be properly organized. It is also an opportunity to see more of the players.

Be upbeat, enthusiastic and have pride. If the coach is gung-ho, the team will be, too.

Give positive feedback - give positive feedback - give positive feedback. This cannot be emphasized enough. Make an effort to encourage every player during the practice session. What people are told, they tend to believe.

Create a non-pressure practice environment. It's natural to make mistakes and o.k. to fall or miss a pass.

Develop confidence and skills simultaneously. The fine line is that young people need to do things they do and don't do well.

Never use profanity and refrain from sarcasm.

Maintain self-control and professionalism when disciplining players. A reprimand or punishment should never ridicule or demean a child. Punish the act, not the person. But if the situation warrants it, have the player spend some "time out" on the bench.

Since a disciplined environment is essential to a quality practice, coaches must possess the courage and conviction to act on disciplinary problems. Be fair and consistent in approach and don't let things escalate.

Coaches who chase players around the ice ordering them to "skate here, skate there," etc. are doing them a disservice. This is inappropriate behavior. Players must feel comfortable so that they can make their own decisions.

Never abuse the responsibility that goes with the position. Macho coaches who talk tough and scream negatives at players stain the profession. It makes what should be a good experience for young people, a bad one, and might run them right out of the game.

A sense of humor is a wonderful quality. It shows humanness. Players respond to coaches who enjoy the whimsical side of life.

Ask questions of players. Inquiries keep them involved, attentive, and reinforce learning.

Allowing team members to partake in some decision making shows respect for their knowledge. It also makes them more likely to react cooperatively to team rules, etc.

The coach should tell players why certain things are being done. If they understand the reason for doing something, players will usually respond with more enthusiasm. Encourage them to ask questions, but obviously with certain limitations.

Always remember that a coach is in a position to be a very positive role model. Children will observe their every move. Set a great example.

Be patient with players.

Develop People.

Practice Discipline

Insist on punctuality.

Everyone needs to be at practice. Naturally, there will be some absences, but instill the importance of being present. (Of course, if the practices are fun, absenteeism will be less of a factor.)

Players are not allowed to leave the ice without permission.

When the whistle blows, everything stops immediately. The obvious exception to this is when a whistle is used to start play.

Team members must move quickly and systematically from drill to drill.

Players cannot be allowed to shoot pucks haphazardly at the boards or net before, after, or during a drill. This type of action can erode the disciplined environment necessary for a quality practice.

Outward expressions of frustration on the part of players is taboo. Slamming sticks, swearing, verbal abuse of a teammate, looks of disgust, etc. cannot be tolerated.

During practice, abide by the rules of the game. Coaches should teach players to perform without taking needless penalties.

If parents attend practice, they should watch from the stands, not the bench area, as it can be distracting.

It is best to limit sessions to players and coaches, unless assistance is needed. Allowing others to skate is often disruptive.

Practice discipline carries over to game discipline.

Proper Instruction

An ideal practice length is 60-90 minutes. Children under 10 years old are better off skating an hour.

Follow the practice plan closely, but it is permissible and sometimes necessary to make adjustments on the ice. On occasion, drills will be omitted. Conversely, a coach may spontaneously come up with an exercise to improve practice. Be flexible.

Explain the drill so it is decipherable to the player. Instructor demonstrations are critical. If the drill or skill warrants demonstration, be exact in the presentation.

Always face the group when speaking, or when talking during a demonstration. Coaches are often unaware that they are not always heard.

At times, have the kids listen on one knee to gain their undivided attention. Occasionally, it is nice when coaches themselves address the team from one knee; a degree of subtle intimacy and identification is fostered.

The old adage KISS (keep it simple, stupid) is apropos. Too much instruction at once will confuse players and hamper learning.

The drill must be done correctly. Stop play if execution is poor, or pull an individual aside who is experiencing difficulty.

More learning occurs when children are having fun.

Teaching/Learning the Game

An effective practice offers a variety of individual skills: skating, passing and receiving, stickhandling, shooting, puck protection, etc.

Numerous skills need to be covered. Unfortunately, many coaches tend to be unimaginative and insular in their approach to teaching. For example, passing drills often involve only forehand passes, but neglect other important puck exchanges, including the following: backhand pass, back diagonal pass, "one time" pass, area pass, lift pass, board pass, drop pass, skate pass, etc.

Individual skill development is the principal focus. Team systems and tactics come later. The priority should be to develop a well-established skill repertoire. Teaching power plays and advanced defensive zone coverages to kids is the proverbial cart before the horse.

When introducing players to a complicated skill, demonstrate the movement in its entirety, then break it down. Players should initially practice the skill in segments prior to performing the whole activity. Allow them to become comfortable with the skill by executing it slowly, before operating at ever increasing speeds.

In exercises involving teams, balance the groups. This stimulates competition, which challenges skills and makes the activity more enjoyable.

Fun games, such as tag or relay races, can add gusto to a practice. These activities can improve skills, although the rules and tactics are often different. Keep players active by minimizing lines and avoiding games that take long to set up. During these games a player should never be "out" for the duration - there must be a means to quickly return to action.

Insist that players "execute in motion." Drills performed at half speed do not fully promote skill development. Players must display good work habits to insure improvement in their play.

Do drills both ways. If a full ice, 1 on 1 exercise starts in both directions out of diagonally opposite corners, then corners should be changed half way through. Otherwise, forwards only attack the net from one side, and defensemen mostly pivot in one direction.

Many exercises require movement at various angles in order to develop complete hockey players. A linear 2 on 0 down one side of the ice is a decent passing drill, but has limitations. A 2 on 0 with players skating in all directions has greater promise for strengthening passing skills; with "Drill Enhancers" (see below) even more skill development results.

An effective practice involves some drills that feature the following: "High tempo for a short duration, in a confined area." A high tempo improves skills and makes the exercise game-like. A short duration insures that fatigue does not set in, which can detract from performance and result in poor execution. Operating in a confined area challenges and focuses the player and increases the pace.

Use "Drill Enhancers" to emphasize a teaching point or to make the drill more challenging. Drill Enhancers include cones, chairs, jumps, etc., which provide resistance. A coach can act in the same capacity by intercepting passes. Players coming from opposite directions, as in intersecting 2 on 0's, also serve as enhancers.

Developing the ability to "think the game" is critical. Young players must learn to "Read and React." An individual who reads and reacts well to a situation on the ice anticipates the play and reacts by making the proper decision. Coaches need to develop problem solvers by building thinking skills into the drills.

Players should not be limited to one position, such as a right wing or right defenseman. This slows development and gives the player a narrow view of different roles. Participating at all positions in practice enhances individual skills and allows the child to learn the total game.

Coaches should place special emphasis on teaching offensive skills and concepts to young players. This takes longer to master than the defensive aspect, because offense requires more skill. If a player has the will, defense can be honed at an older age. Good offensive skills take years to develop.

Hockey is a transition game. Offense to defense. Defense to offense. Often the puck is up for grabs, with neither team actually in possession. On other occasions a team with the puck will suddenly change direction as in regrouping. It is therefore important to include drills that place players in transitional situations.

Neutral ice play should be encouraged. Unfortunately, many coaches view the neutral zone simply as a space to pass through en route to an end zone. Players should be taught to use neutral ice as a staging area for attacking the opponents' end. The intent is to control the puck. Dumping is an option, but it often means giving up possession, and does little to improve skills.

Although specific team systems are for older players (probably over 12), young people can begin learning at an early age that playing the game takes a collective group effort. Offensive team play as well as defensive team play is based on coordination of effort - teammates support each other. The puck must be shared among six (yes, six) players on offense and when it is lost, everyone helps (defensively) to regain possession.

Don't systematize players too much or over-coach them. Too much regimentation detracts from the intuitive process. Team play must not be governed by lanes or rigid positional responsibilities, but rather by concepts, such as that of "support overriding positional play"; i.e. a player can skate anywhere to provide a pass option for a teammate. Allow for creative expression. Ultimately it makes the player more effective and it often makes the game more interesting and fun.

Let players play. Cross-ice games are especially enjoyable. This format on a smaller surface allows for more "hands on" participation as individuals get to stickhandle, pass and score goals, while staying on the ice longer.

Miscellaneous

Good ice is nice. Let the ice freeze up and if working with older age groups, save drills that chop it up for the end of practice.

Every team should have a manager (stickboy or girl). It makes things easier on the coaching staff.

Hockey is for everyone. Invite all sectors of the community to become involved in the sport.

Encourage players to supplement their practice time by playing pond hockey. There are few activities as exhilarating as an outdoor skate on natural ice.

Conditioning drills including repeated sprints, push-ups and aerobic skating, should be minimized. Formal conditioning is for older players. Use the ice time for skills. If the practices are active, enough conditioning will result.

Practice is a "proving ground as well as a training ground." Emphasize to players that a hearty, game-like effort is expected. A good performance in practice benefits the individual and those around.

Wrap up each practice by bringing the team together for a few words of encouragement following the last drill.

Primary among the values that should be imparted is the need for teamwork. Players have to learn that they are dependent on each other and that everyone has something to contribute to the group.

Players respond best to enthused coaches who appear knowledgeable and organized, especially if they perceive that their leader cares about them.

Practices must be oriented towards developing individual and team skills, more than to win games.

Enjoy.

20 PRACTICES

"All too often we are giving our young people cut flowers when we should be teaching them to grow plants. We are stuffing their heads with the products of earlier innovation rather than teaching them to innovate. We think of the mind as a storehouse to be filled when we should be thinking of it as an instrument to be used."

-John W. Gardner
Psychologist/Educator
Harvard University

INTRODUCTION

The 20 practices that follow the "Legend" are the main focus of <u>Pass The Biscuit</u>. Drills have been selected that are best suited for children ages 10-13. Many of them are also appropriate for both younger and older age groups. And, quite frankly, there are exercises interspersed among the practices that will be too advanced for certain 10-13-year-olds. Designing practices catering to young people of different ages and abilities is no easy task, but an effort has been made to achieve that end.

The ideal number of skaters for the practices is 15-25. For larger groups, some drills can be altered or omitted. A case in point would be Practice #3, "2 High Skills Drills." It would be inappropriate to present these exercises to a group of 35 skaters; the players would spend too much time in line, and consequently, very little time actively participating in the drill.

Each practice is devised for one hour. Since many rinks operate on a "50 minute hour," adjustments may have to be made. There is an estimated time period for each drill, but the manner in which the 20 practices are used is subjective, and therefore actual time spent is up to the discretion of the coach. A particular practice plan can be followed verbatim, or selected drills can be chosen from the lesson plan. Because the sessions are designed for young people at different levels, the practices are only semi-progressional, so one practice may be chosen over another. Also, note that even if an attempt is made, it will be difficult for some teams to fit all the drills into the hour, which is fine. The important thing is to benefit from as many drills as possible.

The practices are designed to develop individual and team skills, rather than team systems. Another goal is to encourage player creativity. And, since the game of hockey ultimately is meant to be fun, a primary objective of these practices is to do just that - have fun.

The following guidelines will aid the coach in interpreting the 20 practice sessions:

1) The "Skating/Warm-Up" section is in the back of the book. It includes flexibility and skating options for coaches to use whenever "See Skating/Warm-Up section" appears in a practice. The format for the "Butterfly Warm-up", "Circular Warm-Up" and "4-6 Lines" is explained in Practices 1 and 2.

2) Some drills include a "note" following the explanation. This serves as a teaching point. On occasion, it will further outline particulars of the drill.

3) The "3 Stations" consist of dividing the team into three equal groups. Each coach runs the same drill for all three groups. If fewer than 15 players are present, or less than three coaches, then forgo one station. Every 6-7 minutes a whistle sounds, and players rotate quickly to a new station.

4) Whenever "Both Ends-2 Drills" is noted, the team is split in half and each group does the two assigned drills at their respective ends. At other times, per instruction, split up and do just one drill at both ends.

5) Practice #2, "1 on 1 Keep Away" involves a 30 sec.//1:2 work/rest ratio. This simply means that players execute for 30 seconds and rest for 60 seconds, while others operate. A 1:1 ratio involves work for 30 sec. and rest for 30 sec.

6) "Cross-Ice Games" are pure fun, not stressful. It will often be necessary to use cones for nets.

7) As was mentioned, every drill must be done both ways. For example, Practice #1, "Tracking And Shoot" needs to be performed out of both corners, and players should change direction half way through "1 on 0 Super Flow."

8) In many drills it is explained when the next player(s) in line starts. If it's not stated, the coach must indicate when the next player goes. A central whistle can also be used to start one or more lines. Either way, a coach should monitor each line.

9) In one-way drills that begin at one end and finish at the other, as in "Skating The Circles" (Practice #3), a new line starts at the finish end.

10) This book does not cover goaltending, but it is critical that coaches give the goalies considerable attention and instruction. A good opportunity to work with them is during exercises that do not include shooting. However, they must participate in all skating drills. Additionally, at the outset of practice, goalies should receive some warm-up shots. At the very least, have players shoot from the outside during the first drill.

The following variations can be added to challenge skating, puckhandling, transitional and thinking skills. These twists can enhance many of the drills that appear in the 20 Practices:

1) Perform part of a drill on one leg.

2) No slap shots for an entire practice.

3) Use the colored pucks from Practice #13, "Pass The Biscuit," for other drills to promote different types of passes.

4) During an offensive rush drill (3 on 0, 2 on 1, etc.) have players perform an agility move upon crossing the red or blue line - jump, drop to knees, 360°, etc.

5) Have players suddenly change direction during the drill when a whistle sounds. With a second whistle the players can quickly return to their original direction of travel.

6) Add an extra puck or two to passing drills. For example, do a 3 on 0 with two pucks.

Exercises involving a coach's pass:

7) Pass so a player must change speed or direction to control the puck.

8) Pass so all players must turn back. For example, on a 2 on 1, when players start up ice, slide the puck so the offense must circle back to retrieve it. The defenseman must also adjust.

9) Flip the puck so it must be controlled.

10) Pass the puck firmly to develop "soft hands" and acute concentration.

LEGEND

Player(s)	X 's & O 's	Backwards Skating	= = = = =
Coach(s)	©	Pass	- - - - ▶
Puck(s)	∴	Drop Pass	⊼
Cone(s)	△ △ △	Shot	=▶
Forward Skating	⟶	Defensive Play	⊢
Puck Carrier	∿∿∿▶	Stop	= or ‖

(7min.) BUTTERFLY WARM-UP

Skate as diagrammed without pucks and veer right or left at (A) end. Perform flexibility and skating exercises between blue lines. See Skating / Warm-Up section for options.

Butterfly Warm-Up

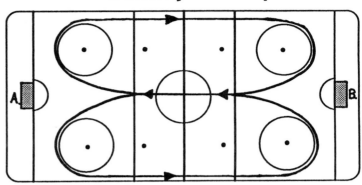

(10-12 min.) 4-6 LINES

Players line up on goal line. Number of lines depends on size of team. On coach's signal, first player in each line performs assigned exercise to just beyond far blue line - glide to finish. Begin corresponding lines at opposite end. When players reach near blue line, next group starts.
See Skating / Warm-Up section for options.

4-6 Lines

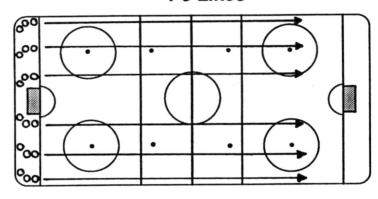

NOTE: In order that the exercises (stops, pivots, etc.) are worked on equally, to both sides, do them an even number of trips down ice.

(10 min.) STICKHANDLING EXERCISES

While players handle puck, coach leads group through the following:

1. Stationary stickhandling emphasizing narrow (puck side to side 6 -12") and wide (2 - 3') dribbles

2. Look at ceiling, over shoulder, call out coach's finger signal, etc.

3. Wide and narrow dribble - top hand only. Next, pull bottom hand up next to top hand.

4. Figure "8" Fashion around gloves as diagrammed.

Stickhandling Exercises

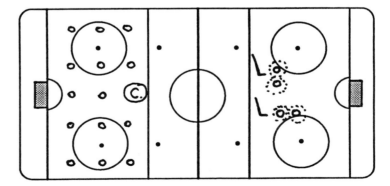

NOTE: Hockey position: elbows away from body, relaxed wrists, peripheral vision, rhythmic motion - don't slap at puck.

(20 min.) 3 STATIONS

A.) CROSS-ICE GAME

Split players into 2 teams and play shinny.

NOTE: To insure active participation introduce this and other exercises quickly so players can get started.

A: Cross-Ice Game

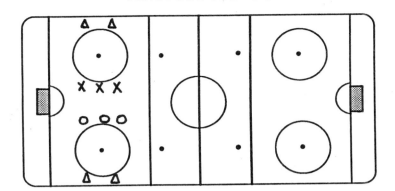

B.) AGILITY PASSING IN PAIRS

Players 8 - 10' apart. After receiving pass make quick moves in all directions - jump up and down, drop to knees, do a somersault, 360°, etc. Do 2 - 3 of the suggested activities at high intensity for 5 seconds in a small area. Pass back to partner.

NOTE: Stick to stick passes, slide puck with authority, receiver presents target.

B: Agility Passing In Pairs

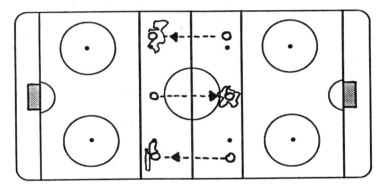

C.) TRACKING AND SHOOT

Coach rims puck around boards. Player tracks it down using the shortest route, turns toward middle of ice and quickly returns for a shot on net.

NOTE: Player reads path of puck and reacts by adjusting route (angle) according to speed of puck.

C: Tracking And Shoot

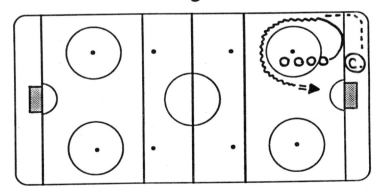

(5 min.) 1 ON 0 SUPER FLOW

Everyone circles rink at 1/2 speed. On whistle, sprint to nearest corner, pick up puck and skate hard in same direction. At next whistle, pass puck in nearest corner, etc. Whistle sounds every 30 sec. Coaches provide resistance in neutral zone.

1 On 0 Super Flow

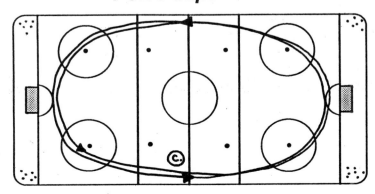

(5 min.) CIRCULAR WARM-UP

Skate around pulled out nets, performing flexibility and skating exercises between blue lines. See Skating / Warm-Up section for options.

Circular Warm-Up

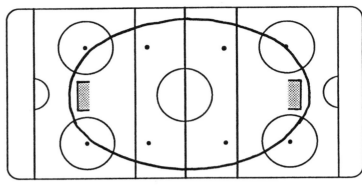

(5-7 min.) PAC MAN

Execute tight turns around face off dots, with pucks. When player rounds 2nd dot, next player starts.

NOTE: Round off slightly before reaching dot - as a baseball player rounds a base. On the tight turn, both skates are initially on the ice. Inside foot glides on strong outside edge and carries most of the weight. Outside skate is on inside edge and pushes.

Pac Man

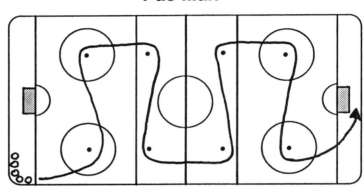

(5-7 min.) DEKE THE DOTS

Deke each faceoff dot and return on the opposite side. When player reaches 2nd dot, next player starts.

NOTE: Use different moves (forehand & backhand shifts, slip through, etc.). Key to deking is feigning (changing speed and direction, look away, body fake, etc.). Accelerate out of deke.

Deke The Dots

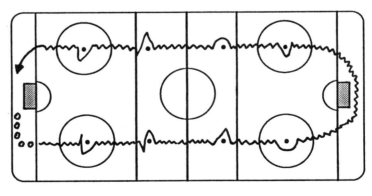

(5-7 min.) CIRCLE JAMS

Three players skate in all directions inside circle "A" with pucks for 10-15 seconds. On whistle, "A" moves to "B" and next three in line to "A". Repeat.

NOTE: Players keep head up and cut hard inside circles.

Circle Jams

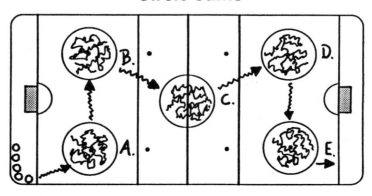

(15-17 min.) BOTH ENDS - 2 DRILLS

Half group at each end.

1.) READ AND PASS (3 vs 1)

X passes to O1 or O2 and quickly pressures O1 or O2. Stationary O1 and O2 read checker (X) and pass puck to O3 (now at front of line). If checker fills lane, pass to partner who passes to O3. If lane is open, pass back to O3. The checker (X) returns to back of line and O3 becomes checker. After 5 passes replace O1 and O2.

NOTE: This is an "International Hockey Centre of Excellence" exercise and teaches players to read the open player and the open lane.

2.) SMALL AREA LATERAL PASSING

Three players pass puck in confined area while constantly in motion. After 7 passes attack net and three new skaters repeat procedure.

NOTE: Promotes lateral passing and fosters a more creative passing game. Emphasize skating in all directions and "eyes on the puck carrier."

(5-7 min.) 1 ON 1 KEEP AWAY

30 sec. // 1:2 Work / Rest ratio. Six players per circle. Two players using puck are involved in a combative 1 on 1 inside circle, for 30 seconds.

NOTE: Puck protection (protecting puck with body) is paramount. Stress importance of competiveness in 1 on 1 battles.

(5 min.) TORPEDOES

Coaches stand in neutral ice with 12-15 small (8") cones. Object is for players to reach opposite goal line without being hit by a cone (torpedo). If hit, player(s) assist coaches, throwing cones from knees. Continue until winner is declared.

1: Read And Pass (3 vs 1)

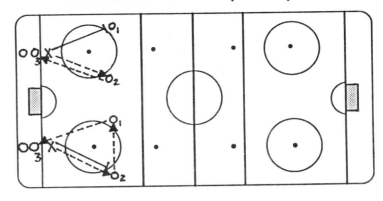

2: Small Area Lateral Passing

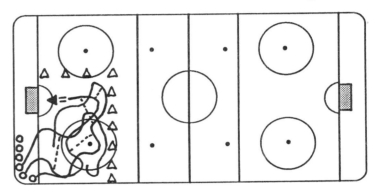

1 On 1 Keep Away

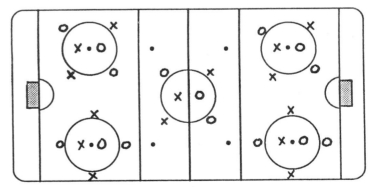

Torpedoes

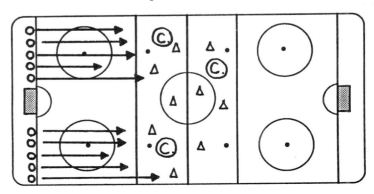

(5 min.) CIRCULAR WARM-UP
See Skating / Warm-Up section.

(10-12 min.) 4-6 LINES
See Skating / Warm-Up section.

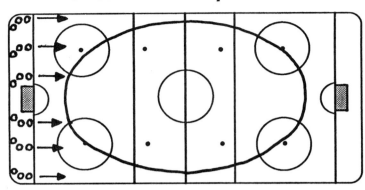

Circular Warm-Up / 4-6 Lines

(5 min.) SKATING THE CIRCLES
Groups of 3 skate without pucks. When trio completes first circle, next 3 go.

NOTE: When crossing over, push with inside edge of outside skate and outside edge of inside skate. If one is neglected, less power results.

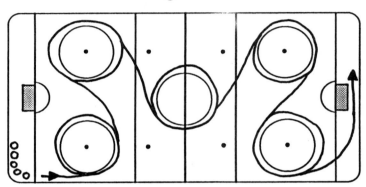

Skating The Circles

(8-10 min.) SHUTTLE SERIES
Players aligned as diagrammed. Receive pass, perform exercise and pass to other line. Move to end of opposite line. Each line does 1,2... simultaneously.

1.) Accelerate to red line and pass.
2.) Lift pass over stick lying on ice.
3.) Figure "8" and pass.
4.) Forward to red, backwards to blue, forward to red, and pass.
5.) Use imagination.

NOTE: Quick feet !

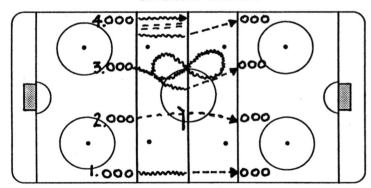

Shuttle Series

(5-7 min.) CONE 1 ON 1

O1 and X1 leave simultaneously from each end. O1 with puck goes 1 on 1 vs X1. O2 and X2 start when O1 and X1 (from opposite end) turn around cones.

NOTE: Discuss 1 on 1 concepts from defensive and offensive perspective. Everyone plays both positions.

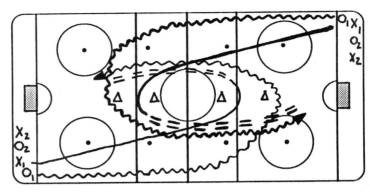

Cone 1 On 1

(5-7 min.) 2 HIGH SKILLS DRILLS

Half group at each end.
Do the following:

A.) O1 and O2 curl to opposite side and back towards neutral zone. Coach passes to O1 or O2 (facing coach), players swing back and attack net 2 on 0.

B.) Same as "A" but recipient of coach's pass shifts back to attack net, other player quickly defends.

NOTE: These are up-tempo drills testing skating and puckhandling skills.

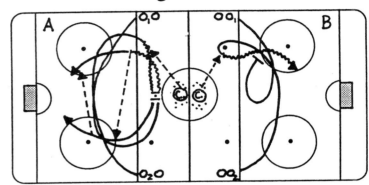

2 High Skills Drills

(10-12 min.) CROSS-ICE GAME

One game in neutral ice. Two games for larger groups. 3 vs 3. High tempo exercise emphasizing 45 second shifts. No faceoffs. On whistle, players leave puck. Next group plays same puck immediately. Emphasize the following:

1.) Constant motion.
2.) Eyes on the puck carrier.
3.) Quick puck movement.
4.) Actively support the puck carrier.
5.) Strong transition game: offense to defense / defense to offense.

NOTE: Encourage players to pass to their goaltender during play. Goalies are increasingly becoming part of the offense.

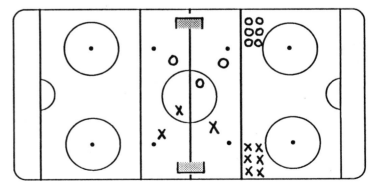

Cross-Ice Game

PRACTICE # 4

(5 min.) CIRCULAR WARM-UP
See Skating / Warm-Up section.

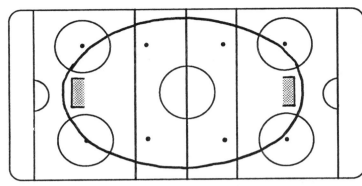

Circular Warm-Up

(8 min.) PUCK CONTROL
Perform the following exercises as an extension of Circular Warm-Up. Skating with pucks around rink, do the following on coach's signal between blue lines:

1.) Imaginary moves.
2.) Stop and reverse direction.
3.) Tight turns toward boards.
4.) Backwards.
5.) Crossovers in all directions.
6.) Handle puck in skates.
7.) Slide on knees while stickhandling.
8.) Board passes to self.
9.) Stop. Three shots against boards.
10.) Use imagination.

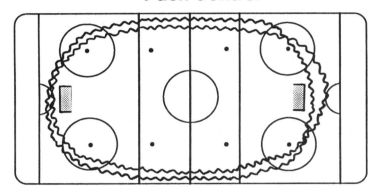

Puck Control

NOTE: May be done with two groups going in opposite directions.

(10 min.) 2 ON 0 COMBOS
2 on 0 to far goal line. The following sequences are done with pucks:

1.) Straight 2 on 0.
2.) "One-touch" passes.
3.) Passing and receiving with skates.
4.) Two-puck exchanges with pucks passed simultaneously (diagram A).
5.) Skate - receive pass, stop and pass - skate (diagram B).
6.) Forward - backwards passing (player skates forward and partner skates backwards).
7.) Use imagination (board, drop passes, etc.).

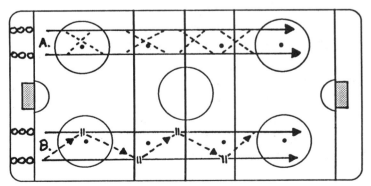

2 On 0 Combos

(5-7 min.) THE DIAMOND

O1 and O2 leave simultaneously with puck from respective ends. Skate course and attack net. When player reaches first cone, next player starts.

NOTE: Tight turns around cones. Shoot in stride.

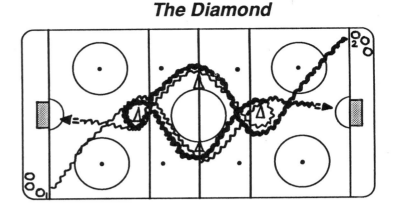
The Diamond

(6-8 min.) CHAIRS AND SNARES

Scatter chairs, cones in neutral zone. Groups of 3 (each player with puck) from both ends leave simultaneously. In neutral zone, move in all directions avoiding obstacles, players. On whistle (30 sec.) go to opposite end.

NOTE: Chairs, cones serve as Drill Enhancers. Players coming from other directions also enhance drill by increasing level of difficulty.

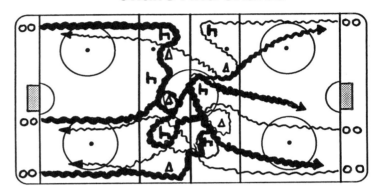
Chairs And Snares

(5-7 min.) SUPPORT STATIONARY PUCK CARRIER (2 ON 1)

Groups of 3. O1 attempts pass to O2 who is covered by X. After start, only O1 remains in place as O2 works to evade checker (X). Change places after two passes.

NOTE: This "International Centre of Excellence" exercise teaches offensive support. O2 must support the puck carrier (O1), working hard to get open and create a passing lane. O1 does not pass until O2 is clearly open.

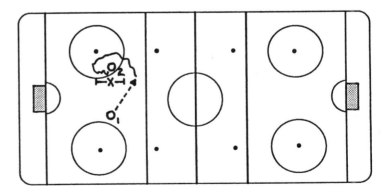
Support Stationary Puck Carrier (2 On 1)

(5-7 min.) GRETZKY TURNS

Skate three hard strides - right angle turn and three hard strides / right angle turn and three hard strides, etc. With/without pucks. Can also be done backwards.

NOTE: Sharp turns should be executed with minimal deacceleration.

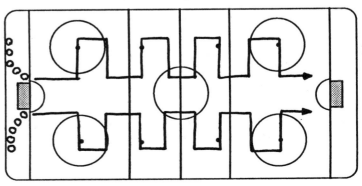
Gretzky Turns

(3 min.) CIRCULAR WARM-UP

Cones and pucks arranged prior to next drill. Short warm-up is conducted in neutral ice without disrupting cones.

(10 min.) ASSEMBLY LINE CIRCUIT

Walk group through entire course before starting. Areas 1,3 without pucks; 2,4 with pucks. Equal numbers start at each station. Players rotate station to station after turn. Keep lines relatively even. Coach or aide monitors each station.

Circular Warm-Up / Assembly Line Circuit

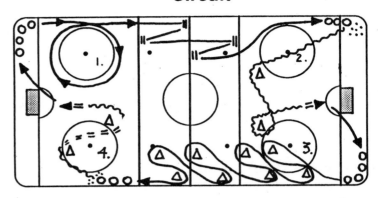

(5-7 min.) STATIONARY PASSING ON CIRCLES

Each group on circles performs the following 4 exercises:

1.) Forehand / backhand passing - no particular pattern.

2.) Pass and replace person you passed to.

3.) One-touch passes to player to the right. After three times around, pass to left. Then one-touch anywhere in circle.

4.) Monkey in the middle.

Stationary Passing On Circles

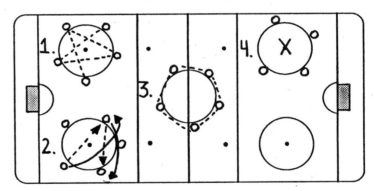

NOTE: Passes should be crisp, hug the ice. Look at target. Passer and receivers stick at 90° angle to the direction pass is travelling. Receiver must cushion the puck by allowing the stick blade to move back slightly during the reception. One-touch passes consist of "one timing" puck so it's on and off stick instantaneously.

(8-10 min.) GILLIGAN ONSIDES

O2 and O3 skate up ice. O1 with puck, goes when O2 and O3 reach neutral zone. O2 and O3 maintain momentum, but stay onsides by straddling blue line, lateral skating, etc. Three players attack net when O1 penetrates offensive blue line. When O1 reaches neutral zone, next players start.

Gilligan Onsides

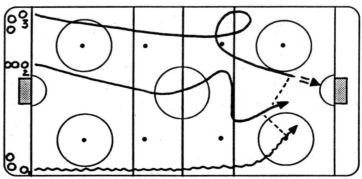

NOTE: Drill is designed to prevent offsides, enhance creativity. Variation would be to allow O1 to pass upon entering neutral zone.

(20 min.) 3 STATIONS

A.) RICHARDSON FIGURE "8" AND SHOOT

Skate through cones with puck, take quick wrist shot. Stagger shooting to protect goaltender. Change lines after shot.

B.) TIMING

O1 passes to defenseman (X), control skates by making a small detour toward the boards. This allows player to maintain momentum and return pass can be received in stride at a good angle. Also, gives defenseman time to gather the pass. After receiving puck, go to end of line.

NOTE: Timing is an important concept. Control Skating (reduced speed) and detouring is necessary if effective, high percentage passes are to be made. The pass must be convenient for passer and receiver.

C.) SMALL AREA 2 ON 2

Two attackers vs two defenders. Coach makes 2 passes to offensive players as defenders cover. After 2 passes, reverse roles for 2 more passes. Change groups.

NOTE: Coach holds puck until player is open to force players to work to get open. Insist on active defensive coverage. Defender must stay between attacker and net, stick on opponent's stick.

(5-7 min.) ARMY / NAVY

Game played in Simon-Sez fashion. Begin on Army Line. If coach yells "Navy" players sprint to Navy (blue) Line. If "incoming" is yelled everyone drops to ice. "Army" go to the appropriate line, etc. Players must obey orders exactly. For instance, when on Navy Line, if coach demands "Navy" any player leaving line is out. POW assignment consists of "outs" marching with stick on shoulder. A coach runs POW camp. Last player left, wins.

A: Richardson Figure "8" And Shoot

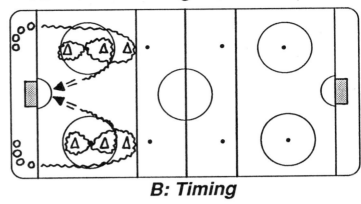

B: Timing

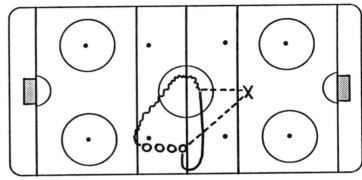

C: Small Area 2 On 2

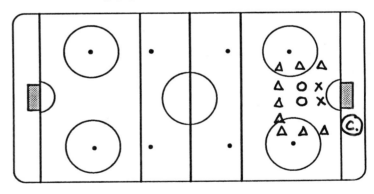

Army / Navy

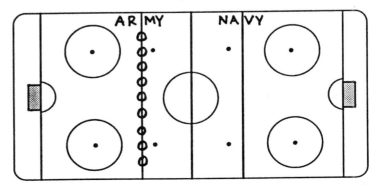

(7 min.) BUTTERFLY WARM-UP

See Skating / Warm-Up section.

Butterfly Warm-Up

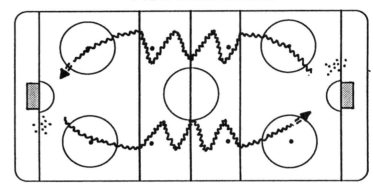

(5 min.) FLOW AND SHOOT

Circle rink with puck. Practice crossovers in neutral ice . Shoot when acknowledged by goaltender.

Flow And Shoot

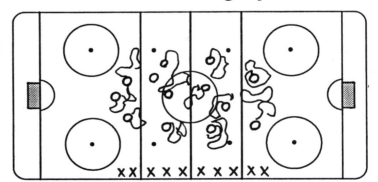

(8-10 min.) RUSSIAN AGILITY

30 Sec. // 1:1 Work / Rest ratio.

Between top of circles, 2 groups do each exercise twice, with pucks. Do the following:

1.) Run in place. Skates high in air.

2.) Leap off one foot, land on other (side - side).

3.) Lateral crossovers with knee touch. Four - six feet to right, touch inside knee, back to left, etc.

4.) Skate in all directions, 2 - 3 shoulder rolls.

5.) Skate in all directions, combination of 1 - 4.

NOTE: Perform activities with high intensity and spirit.

Russian Agility

(8 min.) COMBATIVE 1 ON 1

Coach passes puck a short distance. Two players sprint to puck. 1 on 1 battle (possession may change a few times). Winner passes to coach.

NOTE: Stress the importance of all-out hustle throughout entire play. Two hands on stick.

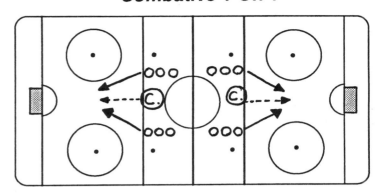

Combative 1 On 1

(10 min.) LOOPS AND REGROUPS

Half group at each end.

Three players break out passing puck throughout sequence. At red line, loop back and regroup with coach. Repeat sequence and end with shot on net. (Coach makes breakout pass from goal line and regroup pass from center of zone.)

NOTE: Regrouping consists of passing back to defensemen to start new attack. Flow oriented teams like the Russians regroup extensively. Introduced to young players, this activity (regrouping) enhances skating, passing and transitional skills.

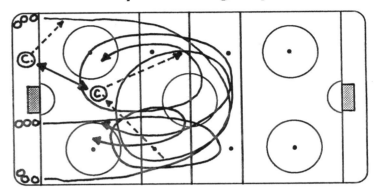

Loops And Regroups

(10-12 min.) HALF COURT GAMES

Remain at same ends from previous drill. 3 vs 3. One minute shifts. O's start on offense. X's must get puck and pass to coach (or player) before attacking. X's then become offense, etc. Offense can pass to coach anytime.

NOTE: Coach makes offense work to get open for pass. Drill promotes transition from offense to defense and vice versa.

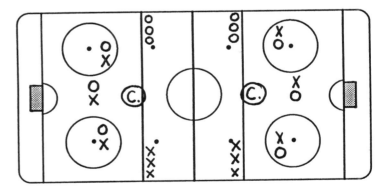

Half Court Games

(3 min.) CROSSOVERS ON CIRCLES

Three to four players per circle. Forward / Backwards.

NOTE: Insist on strong knee bend. Knee bend provides power, lowers center of gravity, counteracts centrifugal force.

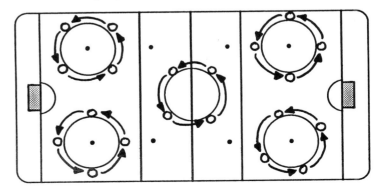

Crossovers On Circles

(5 min.) CIRCULAR WARM-UP
See Skating / Warm-Up section.

(10-12 min.) 4-6 LINES
See Skating / Warm-Up section.

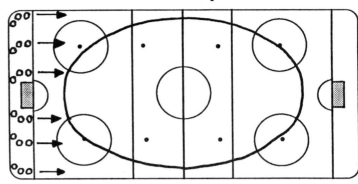

Circular Warm-Up / 4-6 Lines

(8 min.) CIRCLE BACK 2 ON 0
From both ends, 2 on 0 down ice, passing puck. Players reach red line, loop back towards starting point. At blue line loop again, attack far net. When first pair initially reaches red line, next players start.

NOTE: This method of 2 on 0 gets players out of a strictly linear game and enhances skills. Congestion in neutral ice as pairs go in opposite directions is desirable. Keep head up.

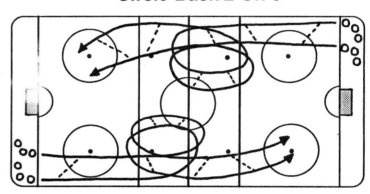

Circle Back 2 On 0

(15 min.) BOTH ENDS - 2 DRILLS
Half group at each end.

1.) SWEDISH SKATE AND SHOOT
Players remain at same ends from previous drill. Skate uncomfortably fast with puck, straight at coach and veer right/left at signal. Shoot immediately upon turning cone. Start when player ahead rounds net.

NOTE: Forehand shots only. Open up body, "shoot against grain," when on off-wing.

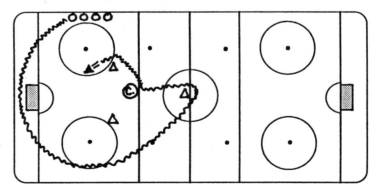

1: Swedish Skate And Shoot

2.) THE KRUTOV

Two players start, one slightly ahead. Skate circle and turn to backwards. Turn back to forward (facing neutral zone) before cone. Turn cone, and first player receives coach's pass. Puck carrier passes to partner for shot. When first 2 complete circle, next pair follows.

NOTE: Passer works "delay" with partner. Delay(s): stop and pass, Gretzky turn to boards (diagrammed), detour to boards and pass. Delay creates time, space and allows puck carrier to find late player(s) entering zone.

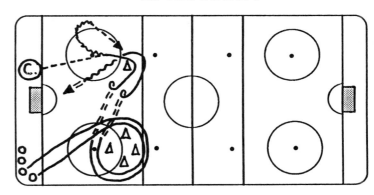

2: The Krutov

(3-5 min.) CAN THE CONES

From respective ends, players bring pucks to near blue line. Three cones are on red line. Two imaginary lines are formed by cones on each side. Players shoot pucks randomly at 3 cones. Winning team knocks 2 cones over opponent's line.

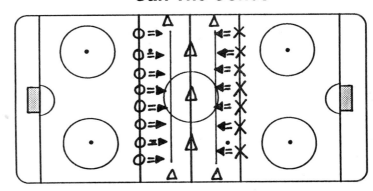

Can The Cones

(5 min.) RED'S MOHAWK

Skate backwards to blue line, hard mohawk turn and forward to boards, etc.

NOTE: Strong inside edge utilization when driving sideways at 90° to boards. One-foot backwards snowplow stop with inside skate, reach to boards with outside foot.

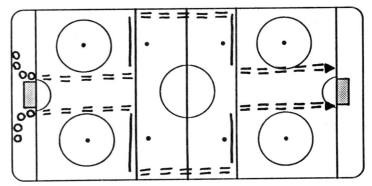

Red's Mohawk

(5 min.) CIRCULAR WARM-UP

See Skating / Warm-Up section.

(6-8 min.) SHOOT TO SCORE

Players line up on blue lines. Perform each exercise twice, with pucks. As skaters pass through blue line, stay in own lane. Do the following:

1.) Forward to red line, stop, attack net.

2.) Forward to red line, stop; on return drop to knees at blue line, attack net.

3.) Backwards to red line, stop, attack net.

4.) Forward to red line, 360° at red line, attack net.

5.) Forward to red line, stop; on return receive pass from next player up, attack net.

NOTE: Practice good shooting skills: head up, quick release, shoot in stride, aim for corners. Low shots, preferably. Hit the net.

(6-8 min.) CHRISTMAS TREE / 2 ON 0

Two players skate course with pucks. Return 2 on 0 with one puck and attack net. When first pair turns cone-2, next players go.

NOTE: On the move, players must communicate and decide whose puck is used for return 2 on 0.

(10 min.) JAMS

30 sec. // 1:1 Work / Rest ratio.

In neutral zone two groups do each exercise 3 times. Skate in all directions with puck. Do the following:

1.) Forward.

2.) Backwards.

3.) 2 on 0 (use backhand).

4.) Deke gloves (bottom hand gloves scattered in neutral zone).

NOTE: Skate hard in all exercises. Keep head up.

Circular Warm-Up / Shoot To Score

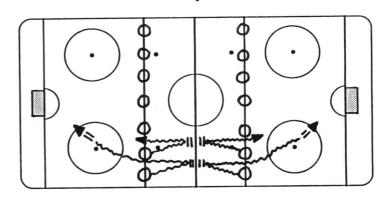

Christmas Tree / 2 On 0

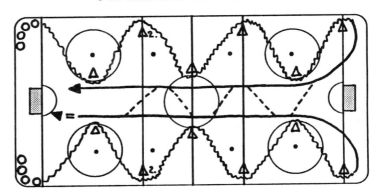

Jams

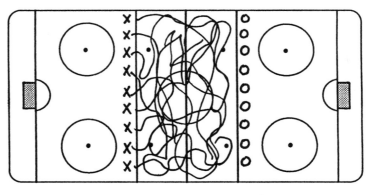

(20 min.) 3 STATIONS

A.) FIGURE "8" RACE

First player reaching puck attacks net. Opponent pressures puck carrier.

NOTE: Good for crossovers, shooting in stride. Teaches trailing defenders to pressure puck carrier.

A: Figure "8" Race

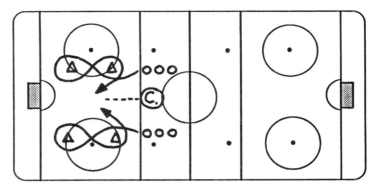

B.) RUSSIAN SHINNY

Goals (sticks) placed 2/3 in neutral zone. Boards and cones are boundaries. To score, pass puck onto stick from within 2'. Everyone plays at once.

NOTE: "Decreasing space, increases pace."

B: Russian Shinny

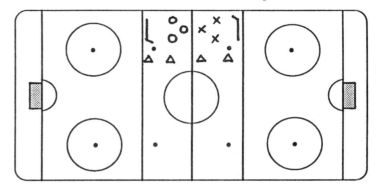

C.) GIVE AND GO

Players assigned numbers. First 3 with pucks skate in designated area between circles and blue line. Coach yells out #1 and works give and go with #1. When #1 is called, #4 (in front of line) quickly joins skaters. If #2 is called, #5 skates, etc., so drill replenishes itself.

NOTE: Player must find roving coach to work give and go.

C: Give And Go

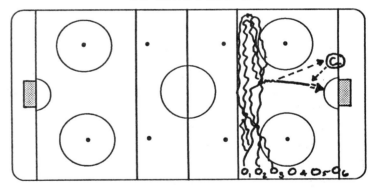

(5 min.) SKATING AGILITY WITH PUCK

Skate with puck to first cone, backwards to second cone, etc. When player is 1/2 way to blue line, next player follows.

Skating Agility With Puck

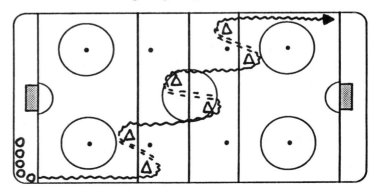

(7 min.) BUTTERFLY WARM-UP
See Skating / Warm-Up section.

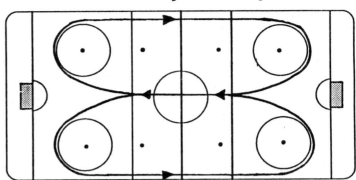

Butterfly Warm-Up

(5-7 min.) COMBATIVE EXERCISES IN CIRCLES
30 sec. // 1:2 Work / Rest ratio.

1.) 2 on 1 Keep Away. Two players keep puck away from opponent.

2.) 1 on 2 Keep Away. One player with puck evades two opponents. If puck is turned over, return to player.

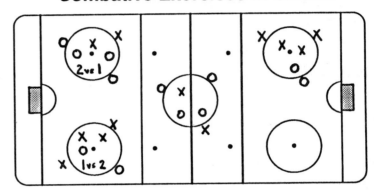

Combative Exercises in Circles

(8-10 min.) SEMLER PUCKHANDLING
In 4 lines. Each line does 1,2,... simultaneously.

1.) Dekes.

2.) 360° (both directions).

3.) Forward past cone, stop facing cone, turn back around cone. Repeat.

4.) Same as #3, but backwards on return to cone.

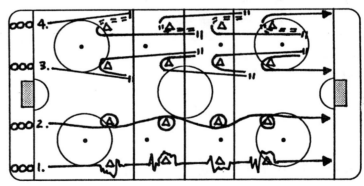

Semler Puckhandling

(6-8 min.) FILL 3 LANES
Three players on offensive rush, receive pass from coach. "Read and React" - fill 3 lanes. Attack net. After pass, next group starts.

NOTE: On the move, players decide which lane to fill. Creates width to the attack. Stress triangulation (shaded area) in offensive end.

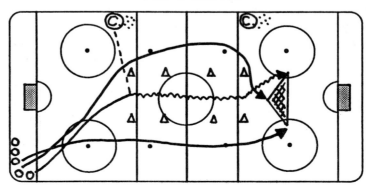

Fill 3 Lanes

(6-8 min.) BASIC BACKCHECK

Both players on knees, wait for signal. O1 breaks down boards. Backchecker (X) defends. Coach attempts to pass to O1, X defends against pass. If pass connects, attack net. Finish, go to other side.

NOTE: Backchecker stays even or slightly ahead of check. Split vision - keep eyes on puck carrier (coach) and person being covered.

(6-8 min.) EARL FULL ICE LATERAL PASSING

Groups of 3 from each end (one with puck) start simultaneously. Cross center ice, six passes between red and blue line. Skaters are in constant motion. After passes, attack net.

NOTE: Encourage creative movement - options for puck carrier by moving anywhere. Head on "swivel" for puck awareness.

(5-7 min.) BACKHAND BONANZA

Players in pairs. Stationary O1 and O2 practice backhand passes and receptions (figure A). On whistle, make backhand exchanges while skating in all directions (figure B). Next whistle, O1 passes to O2, who takes 2-3 backhand shots at boards (figure C), then switch roles. Whistle sounds every 40-50 sec. Repeat entire process 3-5 times.

NOTE: In general, top hand must be centered in front of body, so player is in a position to pass and receive evenly on the forehand and backhand sides of the stick. On backhand, puck is shifted slightly to backhand side, produce spin, follow through low.

(3 min.) JUMP AND STOP

Players spread sticks randomly around rink. Skate in all directions. Jump over stick, land in a two-foot hockey stop. Everyone goes at once.

NOTE: Stopping and agility exercise. Coaches stationed at some sticks, can motion which way to stop, while player is in air.

Basic Backcheck

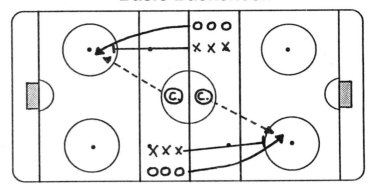

Earl Full Ice Lateral Passing

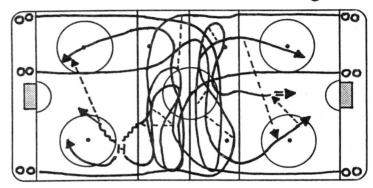

Backhand Bonanza

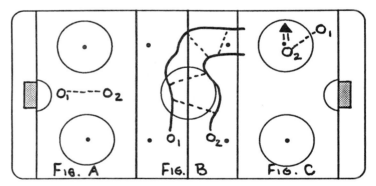

Jump And Stop

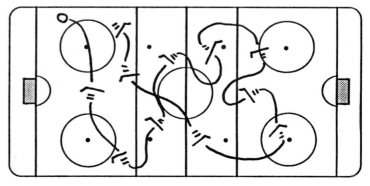

37

(5 min.) CIRCULAR WARM-UP
See Skating / Warm-Up section.

Circular Warm-Up

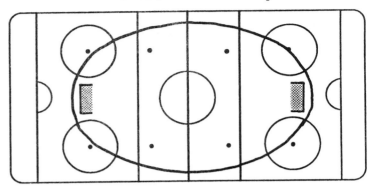

(5-7 min.) 5 CIRCLE DIRECTIONAL
Groups of 3 skate without pucks. Skaters always face one end (Zamboni, clock, etc.) by continuously turning forward to backwards and vice versa. When trio completes first circle, next 3 go.

5 Circle Directional

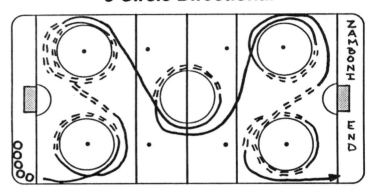

(5-7 min.) BOBBY ORR SPINS
First player in each line with puck, leave simultaneously. Stop facing (B) end. Pivot (turn) toward original (A) end, skate to next stop point, etc. After first stop, next 2 go.

NOTE: The combination of stop and pivot is known as a "Bobby Orr Spin." Orr would often evade a forechecker by this method. Two-foot hockey stops: bend knees, dig blades into ice.

Bobby Orr Spins

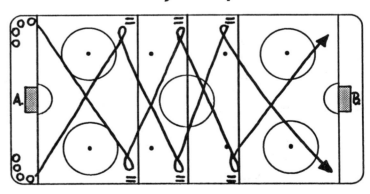

(5 min.) CRAZY LEGS SHOOTING
Shoot 6-8' from boards. Forehand/backhand. Keep feet moving in all directions (360°, tight turns, running in place, etc.), while continuously handling puck and shooting. Short rest every 30 sec.

Crazy Legs Shooting

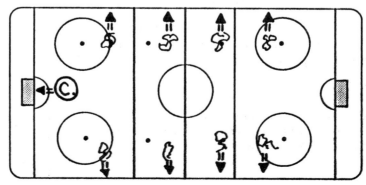

(6-8 min.) PUZZLE 3 ON 1

Three O1's and three O2's skate inside circle in all directions. Meanwhile, defensemen (X's) skate backwards figure "8," and forward around cone to face center ice. After 10-15 sec., coach yells a color (or other reference) and direction, and 3 identified players leave circle. One skater picks up puck, attack X 3 on 1. Other group to opposite end.

NOTE: Players must be briefed beforehand on technicalities of drill. Promotes thinking and communication.

(12-15 min.) CROSS-ICE GAMES

Everyone involved, unlike 3 vs 3, 45 sec. shift format. Goalies and coaches in nets. Play 2 or 3 games at once, depending on numbers.

(5 min.) SKATE TAG

Players (without sticks) skate in all directions, coaches pass pucks at skates. Players zig zag, jump, etc. to avoid puck. If hit, kneel down until tagged by an active player.

NOTE: As in all fun games, for the first minute, miss when passing at skates. It allows each participant to stay involved longer.

Puzzle 3 On 1

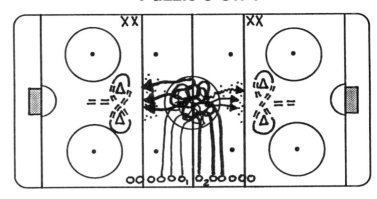

Cross-Ice Games

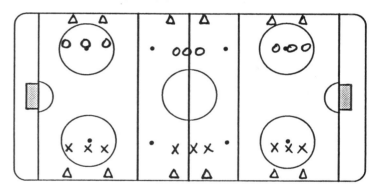

Skate Tag

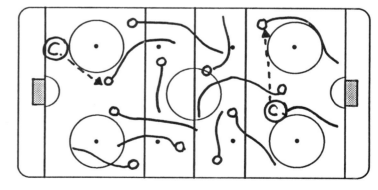

(5 min.) CIRCULAR WARM-UP
See Skating / Warm-Up section.

Circular Warm-Up

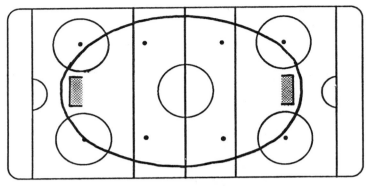

(6-8 min.) QUICK STARTS / FAST FEET
Accelerate to top speed and push through blue line. Return to opposite line. Forward/Backwards.

NOTE: Place skates in "V" position (heels together) for forward start. "Think quick" and start explosively. Push through "comfort zone." (Players get locked into a perception of a top effort, when in reality everyone has more to give.)

Quick Starts / Fast Feet

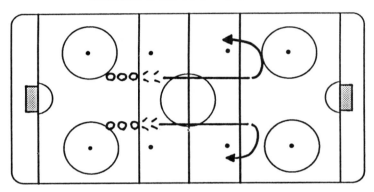

(5-7 min.) 3 ON 0 WHIRL
Three players start, passing puck. Skate to far blue line, circle back to other blue line, attack far net. When trio crosses near blue line second time, next group starts. Start from same side, opposite end.

3 On 0 Whirl

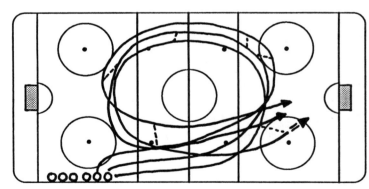

(5-7 min.) ATTACK 2 NETS
Remain in same line from previous drill. Three players start, pick up puck in center circle, attack far net 3 on 0. After quick shot, repeat procedure toward original end. Next 3 go following first shot - results in players skating in opposite directions.

Attack 2 Nets

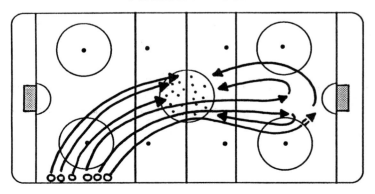

(20 min.) 3 STATIONS
A.) FORECHECK (2 vs 1)

Puck carrier (O1) skates around net. Two forecheckers (X's) go across to intercept. First player angles and separates O1 from puck, partner retrieves puck. X's then work (2 vs 1) from corner, attack net.

NOTE: At older levels, first forechecker takes body, 2nd player gets puck. Younger ages poke check. Cycling is effective in the corner (figure B). O1 pressured by X, sends (cycles) puck to corner and O2 retrieves. O1 assumes O2 spot, etc.

B.) AGILITY SKATING

See Skating / Warm-Up section. (Do selection of numbers 28-39.) Operate between blue and goal line.

C.) JUMP, JUMP AND SHOOT

Skate with puck. Tap puck under stick, jump stick and retrieve puck. Repeat procedure at next stick, shoot quickly.

NOTE: Jumping augments agility, balance.

(5 min.) TWO PIVOT SKATE

Three players skate, without pucks. Turn circle 1/2 forward, 1/2 backwards. Next group goes as first trio completes circle. Start from same side, opposite end.

A: Forecheck (2 Vs 1)

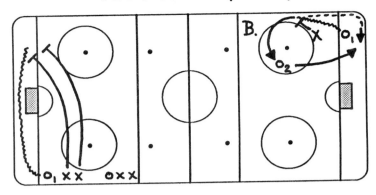

B: Agility Skating

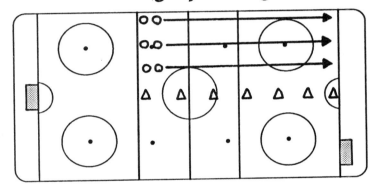

C: Jump, Jump And Shoot

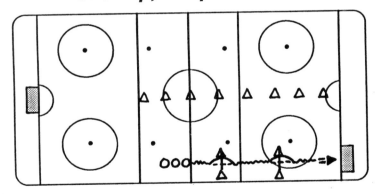

Two Pivot Skate

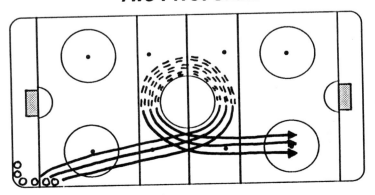

(5 min.) CIRCULAR WARM-UP
See Skating / Warm-Up section.

(10-12 min.) 4-6 LINES
See Skating / Warm-Up section.

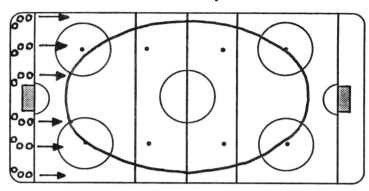

Circular Warm-Up / 4-6 Lines

(3 min.) CONTROL FLYING PUCK
Players in pairs. O1 lifts puck to stick side of O2, 1-2' off ice. O2 knocks puck down, controls immediately. After 10 tries, switch positions.

NOTE: One of many individual skills that is often overlooked.

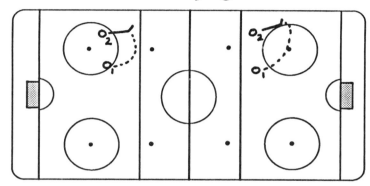

Control Flying Puck

(5-7 min.) RACE FOR PUCK
On signal, 2 players race to red line, stop, skate backwards toward starting point. As players return (without looking back), coach slides puck to red line area. Upon spotting puck, players stop and race forward. First player to puck attacks net, 2nd backchecks.

NOTE: Effective maneuver is to "take the lane," while chasing loose puck. This form of puck protection consists of blocking opponent's lane to puck. Backchecker forces puck carrier to execute in motion.

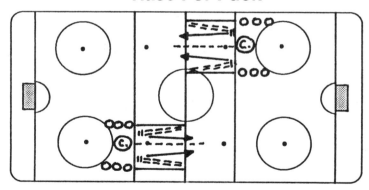

Race For Puck

(6-8 min.) 2 ON 1
Players remain in lines from previous drill. Defenseman (X) jumps out first, takes 2 on 1.

NOTE: Alternate forward / defenseman positions. Forwards should use back diagonal pass, drops, etc. Defenseman avoid overplaying puck carrier, unless certain of getting puck.

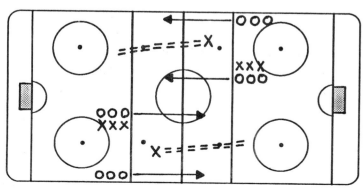

2 On 1

(10 min.) READ AND REACT SHOOTING

Half group at each end.

Coach controls drill from behind O1 and O2. Coach signals X1 to pressure O1, or X2 to pressure O2. (X1 always passes to O1.) O1 reads checking pressure and reacts by passing to O2 (figure A) or shooting (figure B). Switch pucks to opposite side following 8-10 shots. Replace shooters regularly.

NOTE: From "International Hockey Centre of Excellence," this exercise teaches players to keep head up - if pressured, find open player; if free, shoot.

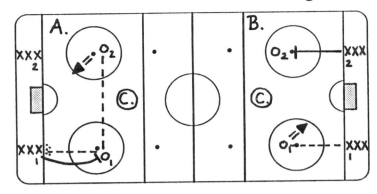

Read And React Shooting

(10-12 min.) 4 VS 4 SCRIMMAGE

Two teams on benches. 4 vs 4 play is continuous. Whistle sounds at 60 sec. intervals. Eight players leave puck, return quickly to bench. Eight fresh players hustle to play. After score, opposite goaltender pulls puck from net, 2 teams skate length of ice to play new puck.

NOTE: Insist on good puck movement - passer and receiver share responsibility for completion of the pass. Everyone tries on the backcheck.

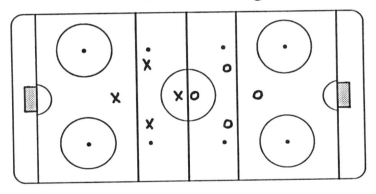

4 Vs 4 Scrimmage

(1 min.) HARD SPRINTS

Two hard sprints around entire rink.

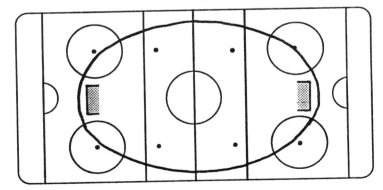

Hard Sprints

PRACTICE # 13

(5 min.) CIRCULAR WARM-UP
See Skating / Warm-Up section.

Circular Warm-Up

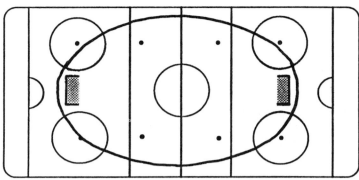

(5-7 min.) BACKWARDS, DROP TO KNEES, DEKE
Backwards with puck to red line. Turn, drop to both knees at blue line, regain feet and attack net. Deke goalie. When player reaches near blue line, next player follows.

Backwards, Drop To Knees, Deke

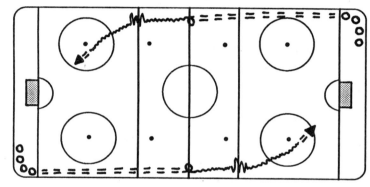

(10 min.) PASS THE BISCUIT
Four players (2 pairs) begin from respective ends, simultaneously. Each pair picks up any puck or tennis ball in circle. In neutral zone skate slowly and make appropriate passes, depending on puck color (see note). After 10 passes, attack net (X's - B end, O's - A end). If another group is at net, players wait and pass in "holding pattern" until goalie is ready. Shot on goal is cue for new pair to start sequence, etc.

NOTE: Pucks are painted certain colors representing a particular type of pass. Paint 4 pucks the following colors: (4) RED - "one-touch" passes, (4) ORANGE - board passes, (4) YELLOW - lift passes (over red line), (4) BLACK - backhand passes, (4) TENNIS BALLS - to promote "soft hands."

Pass The Biscuit

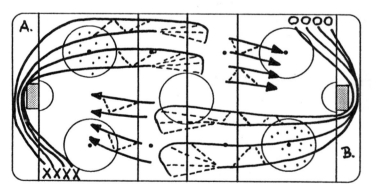

(20 min.) 3 STATIONS

A.) REBOUND AND ROOF

Bench is placed on its side - facing out - in front of net. Player loops around cone, receives pass from coach. Shoot quickly, on ice and follow shot for rebound, flip (roof) puck over bench. Start new line from opposite corner.

NOTE: Emphasis is on following shot, look for rebound. Teaches flip shot over fallen goaltender. Flip shot: blade of stick open, follow through high.

B.) STOP, BACKWARDS AND TURN

Two players skate to respective cones. Stop, quickly skate backwards. 10-15' from cone, turn in direction indicated by coach.

NOTE: After turning, drive hard. Many players turn and coast, which is ineffective against a strong skating opponent.

C.) HALF COURT GAME

See practice 6 for procedure. Only difference - everyone stays out.

(8-10 min.) EDGE WORK

Between blue lines. Skate to red line, back to blue, to far blue, back to red; end up at opposite blue line. Stop at lines, always face same direction. When first group initially reaches far blue line, next players go. Do 1,2... simultaneously.
1.) One-foot inside edge stops.
2.) One-foot outside edge stops.
3.) Two-foot hockey stops.
4.) Forward/Backwards sequence.

NOTE: Most players will have trouble with number 2. Outside edge proficiency assures good stops, strong crossovers.

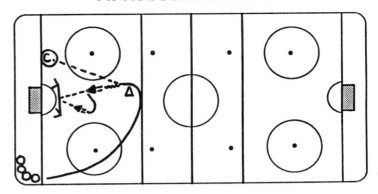

A: Rebound And Roof

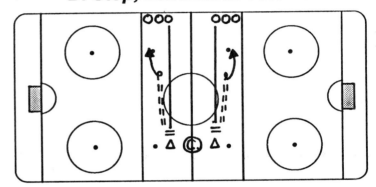

B: Stop, Backwards And Turn

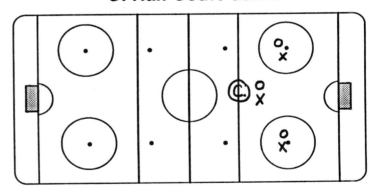

C: Half Court Game

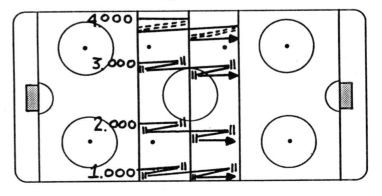

Edge Work

(10 min.) EUROPEAN SKATE

Skate lanes outlined by cones, without pucks. Perform stretching, skating exercises between blue lines.

See Skating / Warm-Up section.

European Skate

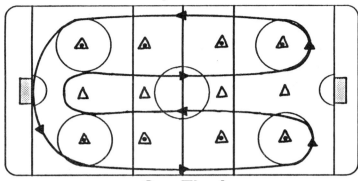

(5-7 min.) SEE THE ICE

Half group at each end.

Coach positioned behind X1 (with back to coach) signals to O1 or O2. Selected player will skate with stick on ice, remaining player with stick 6" from ice. On signal, X1 turns, receives pass from coach. O1 and O2 skate anywhere between blue and red line. X1 turns and looks up ice, passes quickly to player with stick on ice.

NOTE: Read and react exercise. Encourages passer to read open player (stick on ice) and to react by passing. Stresses importance of passer viewing (seeing) entire ice surface for suitable receiver.

See The Ice

(3-5 min.) KEEP ON PASSING

In pairs, skate continuously around rink while passing.

NOTE: Concentrate on backhand passes and receptions.

Keep On Passing

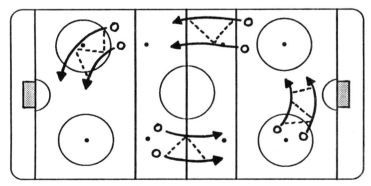

(3-5 min.) WORK ON A WEAKNESS

Players scattered around rink, individually practice a deficient skill of their choosing - a hard move, skating flaw, new shot, etc.

NOTE: Players should be encouraged to practice skills that they find difficult. Everyone should try new things and strive to improve their skill level.

Work On A Weakness

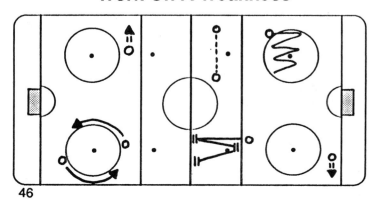

(15 min.) BOTH ENDS - 2 DRILLS
Half group at each end.
1.) SMALL AREA 3 vs 4
Three O's with a puck compete against 4 X's (defense) holding stick blades. One minute shifts. Switch positions at half way point.

NOTE: Defenders (sticks turned around) offer partial resistance, keeping puck with offense. Offense must execute quickly in a confined area. Defenders play body by staying between person being covered and net (no outright checking).

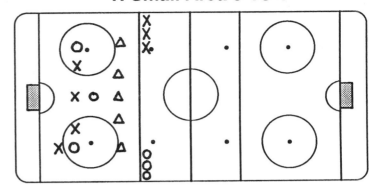

1: Small Area 3 Vs 4

2.) SHOOT AND TIP
Circle far cone, receive pass from coach. Shoot, remain in front of net. Tip next shot, start new line in opposite corner. When player turns first cone, next player starts.

NOTE: Player at net watches shooter, keeps stick on ice to deflect puck. Look for rebound.

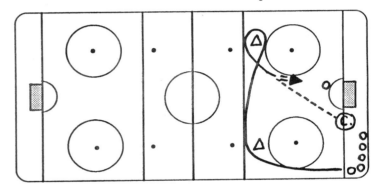

2: Shoot And Tip

(10-12 min.) REVELING RELAYS
Four groups, fewer if short on numbers. Players go when tagged on goal line. Kneel down after turn. Groups A and B use net #1, C and D use net #2. Conduct two relays:

1.) Pile-of-sticks relay: Player at front carries group's sticks. Object - carry sticks around net, return to line. Next player handed sticks, etc. If sticks are dropped, a teammate may assist with pick-up. First group to finish, wins.

2.) Lost-and-found relay: Player at front skates to net, drops stick and gloves inside. Return and tag next player, etc. When last player returns, first player is tagged and skates to retrieve own stick and gloves from net. First group to have everyone re-outfitted, wins.

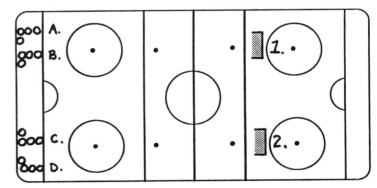

Reveling Relays

(5 min.) CIRCULAR WARM-UP
See Skating / Warm-Up section.

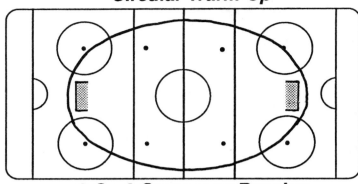

Circular Warm-Up

(5 min.) 2 ON 0 CROSSOVER PASSING

Two O1's skate course while passing. Two O2's start when O1's complete circle B, etc. Can also be done backwards.

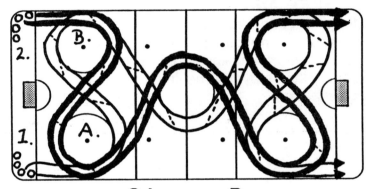

2 On 0 Crossover Passing

(5-7 min.) CRISSCROSS DROP

Players remain in same corners from previous drill. O1 with puck makes drop pass to O2. Players continue around respective cones. O2 then drops to O1. Turn cones, attack net. After first drop pass, next 2 go.

NOTE: The puck must be left stationary on the drop. Timing is critical in the exchange.

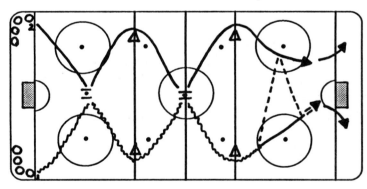

Crisscross Drop

(8-10 min.) BONAFIDE BACKCHECKING

Three players on offense (O's), 3 backcheckers (X's) and 2 defensemen (X2's) start simultaneously. O's loop past red line, return, attack net. X's loop over far blue line, backcheck O's. X2's skate to near blue line, defend attack.

NOTE: Teaches offensive players to keep feet moving, pass and shoot in stride. Backcheckers must hustle to net, even if behind play. If late, arrive at net to prevent second shot.

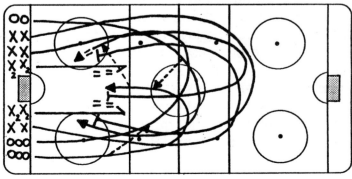

Bonafide Backchecking

(3 min.) BOARD PASSES

In pairs, players make stationary board passes.

NOTE: "Angle of incidence = angle of reflection," when passing on boards. Developing this skill is essential, as boards can act as "7th player."

(6-8 min.) BREAKOUT SUPPORT (3 ON 0)

Half group at each end.

Coach spots puck for O1 to retrieve. Offensive defenseman (O1) pivots to get puck. O1 may feint in either direction with the puck. Forwards (O2 and O3) react to O1 and provide support. Defenseman (O1) passes to O2 or O3.

NOTE: Teaches concept "support overrides positional play"; ie. a player may skate anywhere to support puck carrier. This "International Hockey Centre of Excellence" drill also contributes to timing on the breakout.

(10-12 min.) 3 NET SHINNY

Three teams, each with goal to defend. At start, 2 pucks dropped at mid-ice with 3 centers. No offsides. "A" can score on B,C. "B" on A,C. "C" on A,B. Everyone plays at once.

NOTE: After goal, puck is put back into play without a faceoff.

(5 min.) CATAMOUNT SKATE

Skate backwards to blue line. Turn, full speed between blue lines. Half speed in zone, around nets. Skate hard between blue lines on return.

NOTE: Players pivot to the outside (closest boards) at first blue line - insures work on turning in both directions.

Board Passes

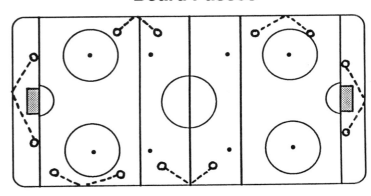

Breakout Support (3 On 0)

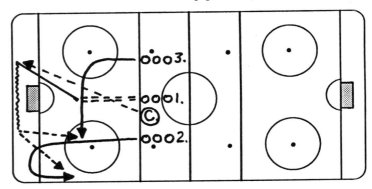

3 Net Shinny

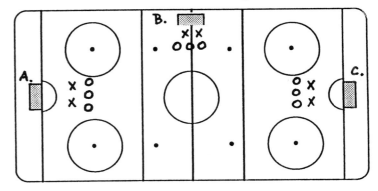

Catamount Skate

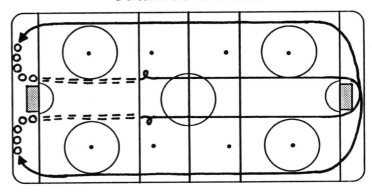

PRACTICE # 16

(10 min.) BUTTERFLY WARM-UP

Butterfly format with emphasis on full speed in shaded area. Half speed forward in other two zones. When departing shaded area backwards, turn to forward at blue line.

Do the following in shaded zone:

1.) Forward.
2.) Backwards (pivot at blue line).
3.) Forward, backwards at bottom of circle.
4.) Backwards (after blue line pivot) to bottom of circle, turn to forward.

NOTE: Concentrate on good, hard crossovers on circles.

Butterfly Warm-Up

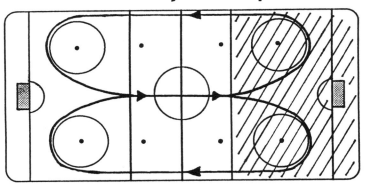

(5-7 min.) THE HORSESHOE

O1 and O2 leave simultaneously with pucks from respective ends. Skate course and attack net. When player reaches first cone, next player starts.

The Horseshoe

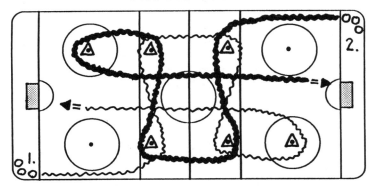

(6-8 min.) CZECH DRILL

Remain in same corners from previous drill. To start, O1 and O2 from both ends skate simultaneously with pucks (O2 goes when O1 reaches 2nd cone). After shot, O1's retrieve puck, pass to O3's. O2's pass to O4's, etc. Four players should always be skating course.

Czech Drill

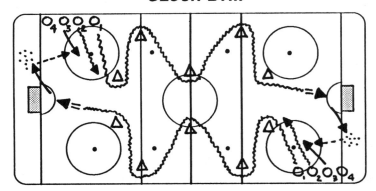

(15 min.) BOTH ENDS - 2 DRILLS

Half group at each end.

1.) 3 PLAYER OFFENSIVE SUPPORT

Three O's covered by 3 X's line up, play opposite coach - between top of circles and blue line. O's support puck carrier (coach) by getting open. After pass reception, defender (X) drops out, puck carrier (O) attacks net. Play until all 3 O's have gone. Switch groups.

NOTE: Pass made only when player is clearly open.

2.) SWEDISH 1 ON 1

O1 carries puck to red line, loops back, passes to stationary X1. X1 does 360° with puck, skates behind net. After pass, O1 swings slowly in corner, receives return pass from X1. O1 loops out to red line, X1 skates to blue line, 1 on 1 results. Switch positions.

NOTE: Good timing is necessary when X1 passes to O1. X1 gains blue line before 1 on 1 to avoid sinking in. Meeting O1 high in the zone allows defenseman (X) to better control play.

(10 min.) JAMS

30 sec. // 1:1 Work / Rest ratio.

In neutral zone, 2 groups do each exercise 3 times. Skate in all directions with puck. Do the following:

1.) Keep turning, forward to backwards, etc. (on whistle).

2.) Tight turns around scattered gloves.

3.) Keep own puck, knock away other players' pucks.

4.) Continuously jump up against boards, sideways. Bounce off, handle puck, etc.

(5 min.) SIBERIAN CENTIPEDE TAG

Groups of 3 lock arms in "crack the whip" fashion. Centipedes (threesome) skate in all directions to avoid being tagged by coaches. If tagged, kneel down until touched by fellow centipede. Nets can serve as refuge ("goul") for 15 seconds.

NOTE: Centipedes are given a minute to practice before game starts.

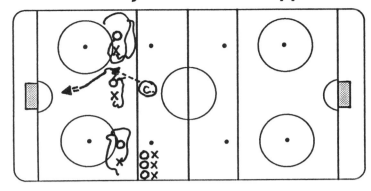

1: 3 Player Offensive Support

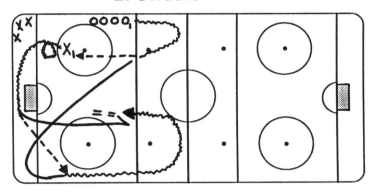

2: Swedish 1 On 1

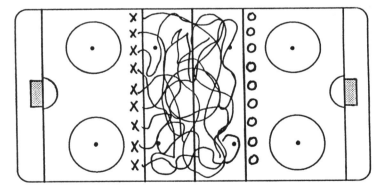

Jams

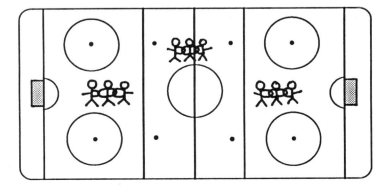

Siberian Centipede Tag

(5 min.) CIRCULAR WARM-UP
See Skating / Warm-Up section.

Circular Warm-Up

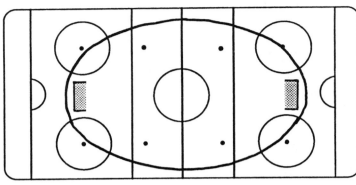

(10-12 min.) 4-6 LINES
See Skating / Warm-Up section.

4-6 Lines

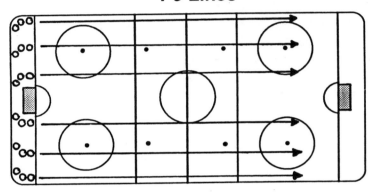

(5 min.) BIG W SKATING
First player skates backwards with puck to cone, forward to next cone, etc. When player reaches first cone, next player starts.

NOTE: When skating backwards, always carry puck to side so it can be passed quickly.

Big W Skating

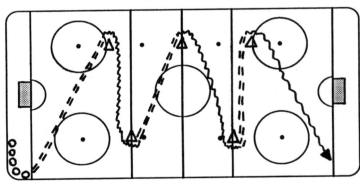

(5-7 min.) DOWN AND 3 ON 0 RETURN
Three players (O1's) break down ice, receive pass from O2 line. O1's return to attack net. After pass, O2's follow O1's and repeat procedure with O3 line, etc.

NOTE: Players create different patterns, swing at good angles, on breakout. Attack offensive zone with speed.

Down And 3 On 0 Return

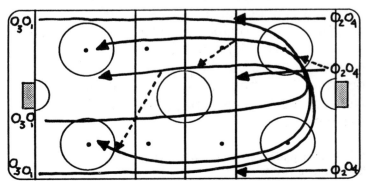

(6-8 min.) NEUTRAL ICE COUNTERS

Scatter cones, chairs in neutral zone. Groups of 3 from both ends (same as previous drill) start simultaneously, passing puck. Regroup with opposite defenseman (X), attack net 3 on 0.

NOTE: Players find openings between chairs, skaters.

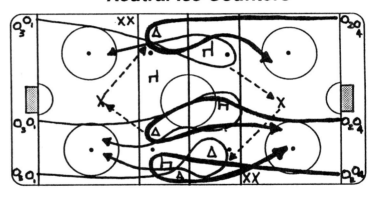

Neutral Ice Counters

(5-7 min.) CURL 2 ON 1

Half group at each end.

Two O's receive pass from defenseman (X1). O's skate over blue line, execute drop pass while crossing, attack offensive zone. X1 skates to blue line, takes 2 on 1.

NOTE: An effective 2 on 1 maneuver is the back diagonal pass (figure B). Puck carrier (O1) attempts to turn X, O2 hangs back. If X commits to O1, pass is made to O2. If X is preoccupied by O2, O1 attacks net. Defenseman (X) aligns with net to contain attackers.

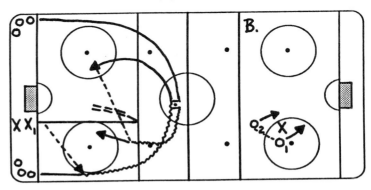

Curl 2 On 1

(10-12 min.) CROSS-ICE GAMES

Everyone stays out as in practice 10. Play 2 or 3 games at once, depending on numbers.

NOTE: For first five minutes, players turn and skate backwards after obtaining puck. Pass or shoot while skating backwards. Exercise enhances skills.

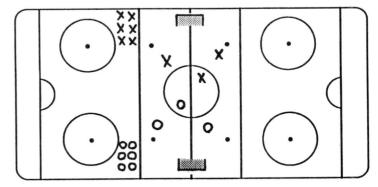

Cross-Ice Games

(5 min.) CIRCULAR WARM-UP

Cones add a new variable to format. Following flexibility: slow down, speed up on whistle. Forward / Backwards.

Circular Warm-Up

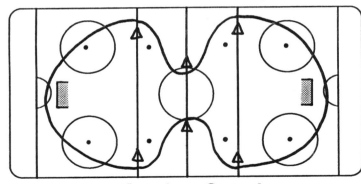

(5-7 min.) GENDRON SPEED

Groups of 3 (each with puck) skate full speed, tight turns around cones. When trio reaches first blue line, next 3 go.

NOTE: Skate "faster than you think is safe." Fast skaters recover their drive skate rapidly.

Gendron Speed

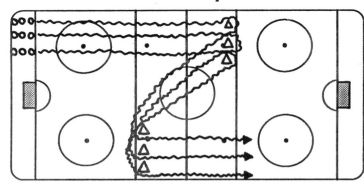

(6-8 min.) O'DONNELL FLY

O1's leave with puck from respective ends, simultaneously. After shot, come to full stop. When O1's stop, O2's go. O1's then backcheck O2's, etc. After backcheck, remain at original end.

NOTE: To add pizzazz, encourage backcheckers to make diving poke checks - without taking penalty - if unable to catch puck carrier.

O'Donnell Fly

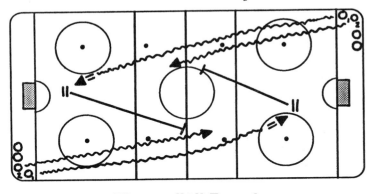

(6-8 min.) FIGURE "8" PASSING

Half group at each end.

Three O's skate figure "8" in same direction, while constantly passing puck. If puck goes awry, coach gives trio a new puck to continue. After 30 sec., next group goes.

NOTE: Good exercise for passing and receiving at varied angles. Passer may be skating in one direction while receiver moves in another. Make plenty of back diagonal passes, as well.

Figure "8" Passing

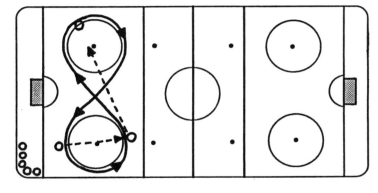

(5 min.) PIVOT AND BREAKAWAY

O1 and O2 lines on either side of red line. Skate backwards from boards, receive pass near circle from next in line. After receiving puck, turn forward and attack net. Passer repeats procedure, etc. (Lines keep moving forward so pass is made next to red line.) O1, O2 lines operate apart from each other. Return to same line.

NOTE: Drills like this that force puck carrier to be agile are especially beneficial.

(5-7 min.) 3 ON 0 TRANSITION

Keeping lines together, coach passes puck 10-15' into (B) end. Three O1's retrieve puck, crossover hard, attack net at (A) end. As O1's enter (A) end, O2's repeat sequence in reverse, etc. Return to same line.

NOTE: Strong transition game a key to exploiting opponents. Turn puck up quickly. Players communicate as to who picks up puck. Spread out on attack (width and depth).

(6-8 min.) KHARLAMOV (1 VS 2)

Two defenders (X's) move to red line. O1 with puck winds up and attempts to beat both defenseman and attack net. Switch positions.

NOTE: In similar exercise the late Soviet star Valery Kharlamov reportedly beat 3 defenders regularly. Drill presents good challenge for puck carrier.

(5-7 min.) HOCKEY HOOTENANNY

Turn on loud music, if possible. Scatter cones, chairs randomly. Set up jumps. Players skate in all directions, free-lancing. In spirited fashion, perform every move imaginable: over and under jumps, drop to knees, crash into boards, slide on stomach, shoot the duck, somersault, run on skates, push puck with head, dance, etc.

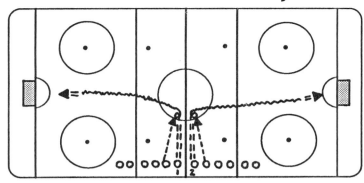

Pivot And Breakaway

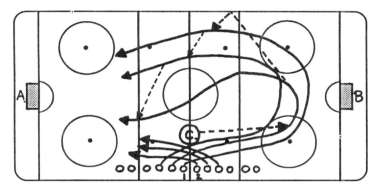

3 On 0 Transition

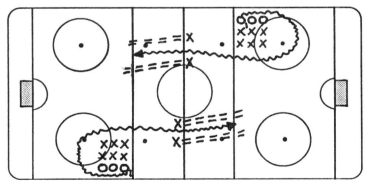

Kharlamov (1 Vs 2)

Hockey Hootenanny

(5 min.) CIRCULAR WARM-UP

See Skating / Warm-Up section.

Circular Warm-Up

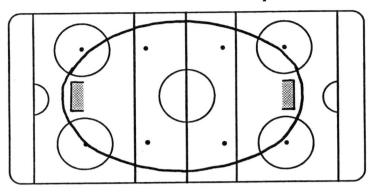

(5 min.) TURN ! TURN ! TURN !

Players perform multi pivots (mohawk turns), forward to backwards, backwards to forward, etc.

Turn ! Turn ! Turn !

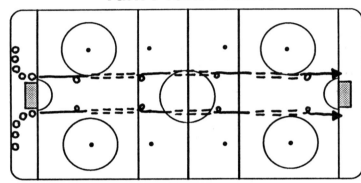

(6-8 min.) STOPS, STARTS AND HAIRPIN TURNS

O1 skates with puck to first cone, stops. To second cone, stop, etc. Puck carrier (O2) makes tight (hairpin) turn around cones. When player reaches first cone, next player goes.

NOTE: O1 will stop and start in one motion. In other words, start in opposite direction before skates slide to a full stop.

Stops, Starts And Hairpin Turns

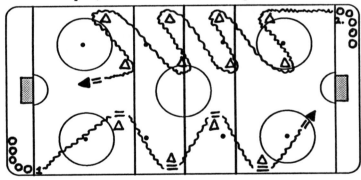

(20 min.) 3 STATIONS
A.) CROSSOVERS / PUCK PROTECTION

Three players skate "hour glass" course in same direction for 45 sec. Stay close to and protect puck from net and coach, when passing through middle. This is not a figure "8."

NOTE: Three nets will be needed for stations.

A: Crossovers / Puck Protection

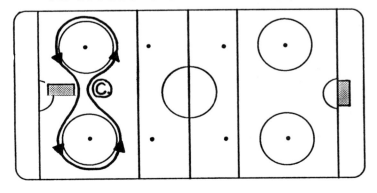

B.) SMALL AREA LATERAL PASSING #2

Similar to #1 in practice #2, but with resistance. Coach attempts to intercept passes, cut off passing lanes. Seven passes before attacking net.

NOTE: Players should make all types of passes: one touch, lift, drop, back pass, etc. Perform at a high tempo.

B: Small Area Lateral Passing #2

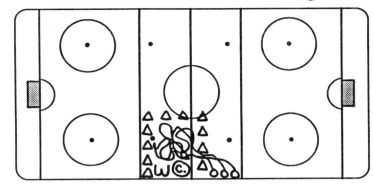

C.) BLATHERWICK "U-O" SPRINT

O1 goes out to cone, skates around circle. When heading toward net, receive pass from coach, shoot in stride. As O1 starts on circle, next player follows.

NOTE: Skate entire course at top speed. According to Jack Blatherwick (U.S. Olympic Conditioning Coach) the most important training for hockey is high speed skill development.

C: Blatherwick "U-O" Sprint

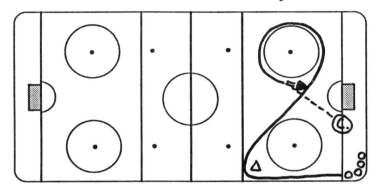

(10-12 min.) FULL SCRIMMAGE

Two teams on benches. Make play game-like, so players can experience "changing on the fly."

NOTE: Regular strength (5 skaters, 1 goalie) per team.

Full Scrimmage

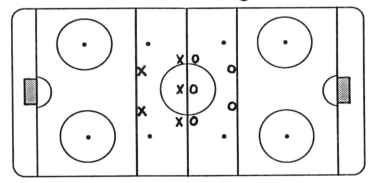

(5 min.) FORWARD / BACKWARDS ZIG ZAG

Two players leave without pucks. Skate forward to cone, stop. Backwards to boards, snowplow stop. Head to next cone, etc. When players reach first cone, next 2 go.

Forward / Backwards Zig Zag

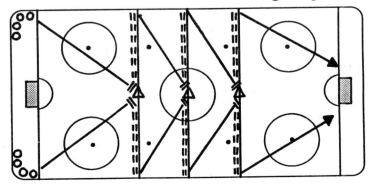

(5 min.) CIRCULAR WARM-UP
See Skating / Warm-Up section.

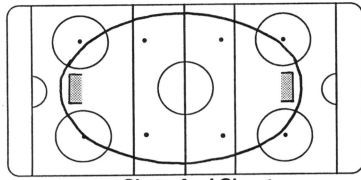

Circular Warm-Up

(5 min.) SKATE AND SHOOT
Skate pattern, crossing over at blue lines. Pick up puck in center circle, attack net. Next player starts when player in front reaches near blue line.

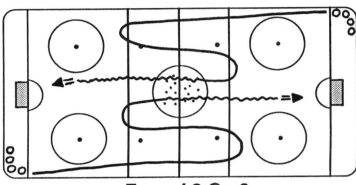

Skate And Shoot

(5-7 min.) FUNNEL 2 ON 0
Two players from both ends leave simultaneously, passing puck. Turn after far blue line, continue 2 on 0 between cones, attack net.

NOTE: Players coming in opposite direction act as drill enhancers. Continue to concentrate on good puck movement during intersection of 2 on 0's.

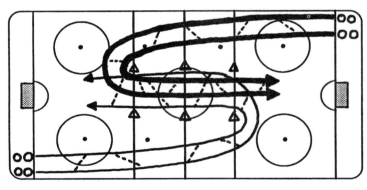

Funnel 2 On 0

(5-7 min.) 1 ON 1 TRANSITION
From both ends, O1 makes "one-touch" passes with X1 (skating backwards). After 3-4 quick exchanges, X1 stops and activates with O1. O1 swings at a good angle, receives pass from X1. O1 then curls back, X1 stops and skates backwards, 1 on 1 results.

NOTE: 1 on 1 drill is improved by adding transitional skills.

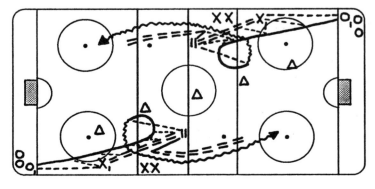

1 On 1 Transition

(15 min.) BOTH ENDS - 2 DRILLS
Half group at each end.

1.) KEEP AWAY
Divide zone in half. Two games of keep away. Everyone plays at once - 2 vs 2 or 3 vs 3 - depending on numbers.

NOTE: Goalies participate along with skaters in this and next exercise.

2.) SHOOTING GALLERY
Two empty nets (if available) against end boards. Hang target (cone, ringlet, etc.) from crossbar, slightly off ice. Plenty of pucks are scattered in blue line area, cones spread around zone. Everyone participates at once. Players retrieve puck, do 360° around any cone, stop on goal line, shoot at either target. After shot, repeat procedure, etc.

(6-8 min.) COMPREHENSIVE OFFENSE
Defensemen (X's) on boards, forwards (O's) on opposite side. Coaches pass puck into respective zones. Three O's, two X's from each blue line, break out simultaneously. Groups skate 5 on 0 (heads up) length of rink. In zone, 5 players pass puck continuously for 20 sec. On whistle, attack net until scoring.

NOTE: Stress balanced support for puck carrier on breakout, move puck quickly. Use points (defensemen) in offensive zone. Passes behind net are effective.

(10 min.) WORLD SERIES BASEBALL
Half group at each end.
O's at bat on goal line, X's in field. First batter (O1) passes puck anywhere in zone (past blue line is an out). O1 skates around cones to goal line on opposite side. X's must retrieve puck, pass to each teammate and score on goalie. If O1 reaches goal line before goal is scored, O's get a run. If not, it's an out. Play 3-5 innings.

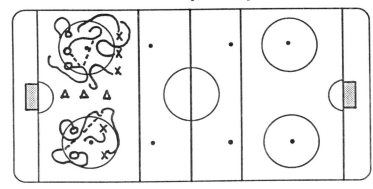

1: Keep Away

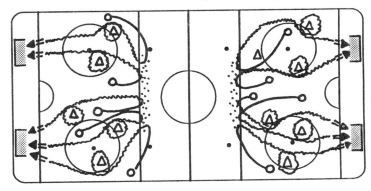

2: Shooting Gallery

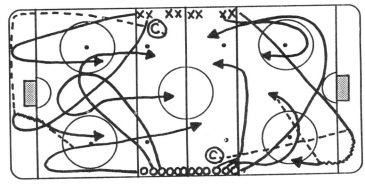

Comprehensive Offense

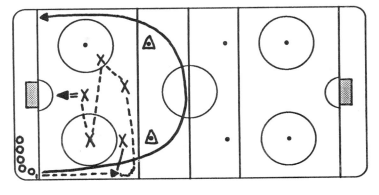

World Series Baseball

SKATING/WARM-UP

"To feel yourself carried along with the speed of an arrow and the graceful undulations of a bird in the air, on a smooth, shining, resonant and treacherous surface: by a simple balancing of the body and by using only your will as a rudder, to give yourself all the curves and changes of direction of a ship at sea or of an eagle soaring in the blue sky; for me this was such an intoxication of the senses and such a voluptuous dizziness of thought that I cannot recall it without emotion. Even horses, that I have loved so much, do not give to the rider the delirium that the ice gives to the skater."

> - Alphonse De Lamartine
> French Poet (1790-1869)

Warming up is a two part process including 1) increasing the heart rate ("warming up" the body) and 2) flexibility (stretching). Allow two minutes of 1/2 speed skating before starting any flexibility work. Flexibility will increase when these exercises are done slowly and held for 10-15 seconds. It is appropriate for flexibility exercises to precede skating exercises. Additional warm-up and flexibility in the locker room is advantageous because off-ice work focuses on stretching and not skating.

The following exercises for flexibility should usually be done between the blue lines and are suited to circular and butterfly patterns:

1) Slowly rotate head in a circular fashion.
NOTE: Helps limber up the neck.

2) With stick held behind the lower back area, locked at elbows, feet comfortably apart and knees moderately bent, twist upper body back and forth, slowly.
NOTE: Helps to limber up the spine.

3) Hold stick behind back, parallel to ice, palms down. Keep arms straight and lift toward the ceiling.
NOTE: Stretches the shoulders and upper back.

4) Holding stick in both hands, gliding with feet approximately a foot apart, keeping the knees slightly bent, gently lean forward and as close to the ice as possible.
NOTE: Stretches backs of legs (hamstrings).

5) With arms extended forward holding stick parallel to the ice, gently kick leg up, alternating, and try to kick the stick.
NOTE: Stretches backs of legs (hamstrings).

6) Execute a lunge position by sliding one foot behind and squatting on the other leg close to the ice. Repeat with opposite leg on next trip.
NOTE: Keeping the toe toward the ice stretches the front of the thigh (quadriceps). Keeping the inside of the ankle toward the ice, while rotating the toe open, stretches the inside of the thigh (adductors) and the groin area.

7) Glide with feet parallel, wide apart, knees straight. Stick in both hands, lean toward the ice.
NOTE: Stretches insides of legs (adductors) and backs of legs (hamstrings).

Skating Exercises

Skating exercises can be done in Butterfly Warm-Up, Circular Warm-Up or 4-6 Lines formats. Most exercises are done between the blue lines. During these exercises it is preferable in most situations to have two hands on the stick with the elbows fluid, responding to the stride for added rhythm and momentum.

The following exercises promote balance, elementary stride development and coordination:

8) Hockey Stance Explanation: While standing still, feet are shoulders width apart with the weight on the balls of the feet, pressing on inside edges. Bend knees and ankles. Knees are aligned over the second toe, hips are over the feet. Bent elbows are away from body, two hands are on the stick which is on the ice. Head is up.
NOTE: There is no position in hockey more fundamental than the "hockey-ready" position just described. It must become an automatic reflex for skating, shooting and passing to be effective. It is a centered position of balance that enables powerful strides, stability in the slot, and agility for precision shots.

9) Perform forward sculls by keeping both feet on the ice, close together, bending ankles and knees. Allow toes to point outward, flowing out to approximately shoulders width apart. Turn toes in and pull feet back together, so each foot completes a half circle. Repeat.
NOTE: Perform sculling exercises slowly and deliberately making sure skate blades dig into the ice.

10) Perform forward 1/2 sculls by sculling with one foot and maintaining a straight line glide with the other foot. Keep both feet on the ice at all times. Keep repeating with same foot. On next trip, use other foot.
NOTE: Most players will have a definite "strong side." It is important that this is noted. Focusing on improving this skill can enhance playing effectiveness and also serve as a measure for personal improvement. Aids with hip flexibility.

11) Balance on one foot, in a straight line, while holding arms extended in front with stick parallel to the ice. On next trip, use other foot. Forward/backwards.
NOTE: Ankles should be stable and not roll from side to side when trying to find the balance point.

12) Skate 1/2 speed.
NOTE: Look for full extension of thrusting leg. Emphasize knee and ankle bend and push to full extension.

13) Skate full speed to far blue line.
NOTE: Be sure the players are keeping their heads up. Going fast is a product of a properly aligned body, working efficiently and smoothly, not a wildly moving body working ineffectively.

14) Perform backwards sculls by keeping both feet on the ice, close together, bending ankles and knees. Allow heels to point outward, toes inward, and heels flow out to approximately shoulders width apart. Pull feet back together. Repeat.
NOTE: Emphasize staying on inside edges with even pressure on both feet.

15) Perform backwards 1/2 sculls by sculling with one foot and maintaining a straight line glide with the other foot. Keep both feet on the ice at all times. Keep repeating with same foot. On next trip, use other foot.
NOTE: Look for full extension of the thrusting foot slightly to the front and side. Aids with hip rotation and flexibility.

16) Skate backwards, alternating the thrust. Line of travel should be as straight as possible. Keep only the top hand on the stick, stick on the ice.
NOTE: Be sure both feet stay on the ice with full extension of the pushing foot. Keep head up. Add alternating backwards crossovers as a variation to this exercise

17) Turn (pivot) to backwards at blue line. Turn to forward at next blue line. Always face the same direction.
NOTE: Watch for flailing sticks. Sticks should stay on the ice immediately in front of the body.

18) Skate hard. At the blue line execute a tight turn held for a full circle and repeat in the opposite direction at the next blue line.
NOTE: Avoid coasting after turn execution.

19) At the blue line, turn and skate backwards to the far blue line. Turn to forward and immediately skate a tight turn held for a full circle.
NOTE: Full circle tight turns require good use of edges, proper weight distribution and concentration.

The following exercises promote better stopping: (It is important to select a wall and always stop, facing the same wall for the duration. This eliminates exclusive use of the stronger side. Emphasize complete stops.)

20) One-foot stops, outside and inside edges. Glide on one foot and stop on the blue line, red line and far blue line. First trip, stop on the right. Second trip, stop on the left. Third trip, stop on the left. Fourth trip, stop on the right. All edges are used. Start the next group when the preceding group leaves the first blue line.
NOTE: Emphasize knee bend and hockey stance position upon stop completion.

21) Use hockey stops. While always skating forward, skate hard to the red line, stop. Skate to the blue line which has already been crossed, stop. (Next group begins.) Skate to the far blue line, stop. Skate to the red line, stop. Skate to far goal line.
NOTE: Be sure both blades dig into the ice, shoulders width apart, producing snow when stopping.

22) Backwards snowplow stops on each blue line.
NOTE: Promote knee bend, even stopping with both feet. Be sure that at the completion of the stop, feet are in a slightly open "V" and remain nearly shoulders width apart.

23) Skate backwards to the red line, stop. Skate forward to the blue line which has already been crossed, stop. (Next group begins.) Begin to skate forward to far blue line, immediately turning to backwards. While skating backwards stop on far blue line. Skate forward toward center red line, immediately execute a tight turn, U-turn as when going around a cone, and skate forward to far goal line.
NOTE: Improves maneuverability and tests the player's ability to follow more complex instructions.

The following exercises deal with edge work and power promotion: (Good command of edges can get a player out of trouble - leading to stronger stops and more forceful crossovers.)

24) Alternating forward inside edges. These edges are large 1/2 circles, three times the height of the player in diameter. Skate counterclockwise on right forward inside edge. Change direction to clockwise when stepping on left forward inside edge. Repeat. Fully extend the leg that pushes.
NOTE: Develops the forward inside edge and promotes better stride position.

25) Skate 1/2 speed to the blue line, then zig zag on one foot slalom style, alternating edges from outside to inside. Change feet on next trip. Forward/backwards.
NOTE: Improves balance and ability to recover quickly.

26) From goal line to goal line, starting from a standstill, zig zag on one foot slalom style, alternating edges from outside to inside. Change feet on next trip. Forward/backwards.
NOTE: This exercise promotes command of the edges, demanding that pressure be exerted into the ice for propulsion to occur and thus, power results.

27) Alternating, 3 step forward crossovers. Referred to as step-cross-step. While curving counter clockwise, step left forward outside, cross right foot over to a right forward inside edge, step on left forward outside. Change curve to clockwise by stepping right forward outside, cross left foot over right to a left inside edge, step right forward outside. Repeat.
NOTE: This is an important drill players often do incorrectly by continually crossing over when a step is required between crossovers. This is a series of steps that quickly and powerfully accelerates the player down the ice. From this pattern, great offensive players add numerous dekeing motions.

The following exercises promote agility and quickness which can aid with development of edges for the creation of power:

28) Dips: Squat cannonball-style while doing a two-foot glide. Forward/backwards.

29) Shoot the duck: While doing a dip, extend one leg straight out in front. On next trip, use other foot. Forward/backwards.

30) "Cossack" dance: While performing shoot the duck, rapidly alternate the feet while staying in a squatted position.

31) Touch one knee at blue line. Skate. Touch other knee at red line. Skate. Drop to both knees at far blue line.

32) While skating slowly, at every line "broad jump" off of both feet, striving for maximum distance.
NOTE: Promotes full extension of leg through the toe and proper body alignment.

33) From a moving start, leap laterally, side to side, as wide as possible, while alternating feet and using inside edges.
NOTE: Emphasizes the connection between extended thrusts and power.

34) Make as many quick "running" steps as possible.
NOTE: Using a running (not skating) motion helps with balance and quickness.

35) While travelling slowly, hop very quickly three times on one foot and then three times on the other foot. Repeat.

36) Stop at the first blue line and face the side of the arena. Perform a series of rapid crossovers by executing step-cross-step, with stick held parallel to ice, extending arms. After completing one crossover, quickly turn and face the opposite direction. Repeat.
NOTE: Entire body must shift very quickly during the transitions.

37) At first blue line, while skating full speed, do a tuck jump, cannonball style, pulling knees into chest. At the red line slide on belly and do a log roll. At blue line drop to both knees and return to upright

38) While skating 3/4 speed, turn continuously forward to backwards, backwards to forward, turning 180° not 360°, as quickly as possible. May be done with one or both hands on stick; each position produces a unique effect. On next trip, repeat in opposite direction.
NOTE: Promotes openness in hips, necessary for proper long stride development and emphasizes that the placement of the stick with relationship to the body creates improved balance. There are many such turns in game situations.

39) While skating 3/4 speed, do a 360° at each blue line. Rotate counterclockwise, by turning forward to backwards, then crossing the foot in front, while still traveling backwards, and turning to forward. On next trip, repeat clockwise.
NOTE: Contributes to rotational awareness (regaining balance and sense of direction) which is key to quick recovery when spinning out of a check.

Addition of puck:

40) Stickhandle down the ice.

41) While skating hard, push puck ahead similar to a breakaway situation.
NOTE: Keep elbows relaxed, and attempt not to over-stickhandle.

42) Stickhandle while skating backwards. Turn to forward at far blue line.

43) At each blue line, skate a small clockwise circle approximately 10 feet in diameter, with strong crossovers. On next trip, do counterclockwise circles.

44) Turn to backwards at blue line while controlling the puck and turn to forward at the far blue line.
NOTE: Demands a moderate level of expertise in doing a turn while controlling the puck.

45) Repeat #18 with a puck.
NOTE: Emphasize momentum as soon as completing the turn.

46) Same as #27.
NOTE: To control the puck, stickhandling mostly takes place in a narrow alley in front of the body, which increases the skills necessary for dekeing.

47) While skating 1/2 speed with the puck, execute a 360° at each blue line.
NOTE: Improves puck control by increasing rotational awareness.

48) Beginning at the red line, slide on knees, while dribbling the puck.
NOTE: This helps to keep bent elbows away from the body.

49) After crossing the first blue line, glide past puck. Quickly turn to backwards in same direction and retrieve puck by reaching it with the stick. Tap puck through legs. Turn quickly to forward and skate hard with puck.

Unusual drills which may be chosen on occasion:

50) Skate in time to music. Alter the rhythm and tempo.
NOTE: This makes every step a planned event. Steps taken because of loss of balance become readily apparent.

51) Skate in slow motion.
NOTE: Reflection on stride position creates body awareness and reinforces the necessity of proper technique.

52) Jump rope.
NOTE: Increases balance and coordination.

53) With a puck, skate the length of the rink with as many dekes, tight turns, stops and starts, etc. as possible.
NOTE: Develops creativity, confidence and agility.

54) Fast starts on clean ice.
NOTE: Look for short, open cuts, which appear as diagonal lines (approximately 45°), with a distinctive wedge impression in the ice. There should be more distance between steps 2 and 3, than between steps 1 and 2. It is advantageous to work with a partner able to readily identify the marks on the ice. Encourage players to lean forward before commencing the fast start.

55) Use imagination and develop other ideas!

BIBLIOGRAPHY

Associate Coaches Manual (1985). Colorado Springs, Colorado: U.S.A. Hockey.

Bercuson, Richard (1990). Low Organization Ice Games. Hockey Coaching Journal.

Chambers, Dave (1989). Complete Hockey Instruction. Toronto, Ontario: Key Porter Books Limited.

Coaching Achievement Program. Associate Clinic. Massachusetts District: U.S.A. Hockey.

Gendron, Red (1989). Bellows Free Academy Hockey Drill Book.

Goals 1&2 (video). Calgary, Alberta: International Hockey Centre of Excellence: Hockey Canada in Cooperation with the Canadian Amateur Hockey Association.

Kingston, George (1979). Developmental Concepts of Offensive Team Play - Peewee and under. Proceedings. National Coaches Certification Program. Level 5. (pp. 153-173) Vanier, Ontario: Canadian Amateur Hockey Association.

Kostla, Vladmir (1979). Czechoslovakian Youth Ice Hockey Training System. Vanier, Ontario: Canadian Amateur Hockey Association.

Orn, Wayne (1980-1984). The Hockey Coach's Newsletter.

Richardson, Bob (1987-1990). Coaching Tips (various articles). Hockey/U.S.A. Newspaper.

Stamm, Laura (1989). Power Skating. Champaigne, Illinois: Leisure Press.

Taylor, Tim (1990). Adding the Offensive Read and React Aspect to your Existing Drills.

Epigraphs
Anatoly Tarasov quotation from Riding on the Roar of the Crowd compiled by David Gowdey, Macmillan of Canada, Toronto, Ont; John W. Gardner from Supervision: School Leadership Handbook by Lloyd W. Dull, Charles E. Merrill Publishing Co., Columbus, OH.

ABOUT THE AUTHOR

Gary Wright is the hockey coach at American International College in Springfield, MA. He also served as an assistant at the University of Maine and as coach at Rice Memorial High School in Vermont. His involvement with youth includes past directorship of a YMCA Summer Camp and a National Youth Sports Program, sponsored by the NCAA. He currently spends his summers instructing at hockey schools.

Julia Sutphin-Tortorella wrote the Skating/Warm-Up section. She is the Assistant Rink Manager and Skating Director at Kennebec Ice Arena in Augusta, ME. She has taught skating to figure skaters and hockey players at all levels.

Bryon Lewis served as the book's graphic artist. A former goaltender at American International College for Coach Wright, he designed the layout and illustrated the rink diagrams. He is pursuing a masters degree at his alma mater and has started a printing business.